DOUBLE SOLITAIRE

DOUBLE SOLITAIRE

The Films of
CHARLES BRACKETT
and **BILLY WILDER**

DONALD BRACKETT

APPLAUSE
THEATRE & CINEMA BOOKS

Essex, Connecticut

APPLAUSE
THEATRE & CINEMA BOOKS

An imprint of Globe Pequot, the trade division of
The Rowman & Littlefield Publishing Group, Inc.
4501 Forbes Blvd., Ste. 200
Lanham, MD 20706
www.rowman.com

Distributed by NATIONAL BOOK NETWORK

Library of Congress Cataloging-in-Publication Data available

ISBN 9781493076062 (cloth : alk. paper)
ISBN 9781493076079 (electronic)

∞™ The paper used in this publication meets the minimum requirements
of American National Standard for Information Sciences—Permanence of
Paper for Printed Library Materials, ANSI/NISO Z39.48-1992

Movies are magic.

VAN DYKE PARKS

CONTENTS

PROLOGUE

Ready for Their Close-Up

Hide in the mirror. No one will look for you there.

LJUPKA CVETANOVA, *THE NEW LAND*

I never met Charles Brackett. He died in 1969, when I was a teen-
ager. But I still spent a great deal of time in his company. When I
was a kid, growing up in the vast wasteland suburb of Don Mills just
outside Toronto, there wasn't much to do, but it was a splendid locale
for reading books and watching late-night black-and-white television, and I was treated to a rather unique experience that my fellow
truants perhaps were not. While wiling away the dreamy nocturnal
hours in front of that magic flickering analog box, I would occasionally be taken aback by the sight of my own surname on the screen
for the writer and producer of many a classic film, shown via the still
relatively new medium of network broadcasting.

There was, in those days, an almost total absence of the specifically produced programming content we take for granted today, and
instead, the newborn fledgling networks would randomly recycle
movies from the early age of cinema for unsuspecting viewers such
as myself. They desperately needed video content, and Hollywood
provided it at bargain-basement rates. When I asked my parents
who this "Charles Brackett" was who kept popping up on-screen in

the middle of my teenage nights, their somewhat innocent suburban response was something along the lines of, "Oh yeah, I think he was part of the American branch of the family who had something to do with Hollywood."

Something to do with Hollywood? He was in fact Hollywood royalty, as well as having been a member of the Lost Generation in Europe along with Hemingway and Fitzgerald (both of whom he knew and helped nurse through their worst hangovers) before coming to New York and joining the Algonquin Round Table along with Dorothy Parker and Robert Benchley (providing more help with hangovers, Charlie being almost a teetotaler), while also serving as the drama critic for *The New Yorker*.

Like other talented writers (including of course, Fitzgerald, Huxley, and Faulkner) he was eventually lured to Hollywood, where he was teamed up by Paramount Studios with a certain recent émigré from Austria, who barely spoke English, to write screenplays for the great film director Ernst Lubitsch.

That particular émigré was in fact the acerbic Billy Wilder, with whom my great-great-grandfather's cousin Charles Brackett had a volatile love-hate partnership that spanned the writing, producing, and directing of some of cinema's greatest screwball comedies as well as classics of film noir. I've long dreamed about the strange magic of their fraught collaboration, and their creative career history situates my first exposure to the realization that films, motion pictures, cinema, flicks, or movies, whatever we choose to call them, were and still are a huge part of the larger history of visual art. They are, in fact, a unique form of painting with light and time, shared together in brilliant darkness, whether they are entertaining and commercially successful or arcane and emotionally arresting.

How do you spend time with someone you've never met? By traveling together through the movies that he made. In a curious way, this book is my own personal version of *Travels with Charley*, except that in my case I traveled extensively far and wide but without ever moving a muscle, via the mysterious magic of cinema. Where did my distant family relative Charles Brackett take me in his distant travels? He took me solely to those special places located in the geography of the imagination, the kind he created as an Academy Award–winning Hollywood screenwriter and producer during the Golden Age of cinema, an epoch the likes of which we shall probably never see again. Together, we traveled in the middle of the night, in the dark, down celluloid roads.

He took me to visit the Ernst Lubitsch universe in *Bluebeard's Eighth Wife*; to Greta Garbo's shimmering laughter in *Ninotchka*; to Claudette Colbert's smoldering smile in *Midnight*; to Gary Cooper's otherworldly coolness in *Ball of Fire*; to the audacity of Charles Boyer in *Hold Back the Dawn*; to the racy innocence of Ginger Rogers in *The Major and the Minor*; to the imperious visage of Erich von Stroheim in *Five Graves To Cairo*; to the claustrophobic nightmares of Ray Milland in *The Lost Weekend*; to the ironic sexuality of Marlene Dietrich in *A Foreign Affair*; to the sophisticated noir mindscape of *Sunset Boulevard*; to the emotional desperation of Clifton Webb in *Titanic*; to the force of nature known as Marilyn Monroe in *Niagara*; to the elegant charm of Deborah Kerr and Yul Brynner in *The King and I*; and many other spots on the map of the heart.

My book explores the dynamics behind the eventual creation of *Sunset Boulevard*, the corrosive culmination of the highly volatile and competitive partnership between writer-director Wilder and writer-producer Brackett, as well as the huge impact of their many other classic films on our popular culture via an intimate glimpse behind the curtain of Hollywood's Golden Age. Brackett collaborated with Wilder on thirteen films between 1936 and 1949, the year they made *Sunset Boulevard* together and won the Academy Award for Best Original Screenplay. It was also the year that Charlie could no longer stand the constant conflict and bickering with his partner, the gifted but darkly disturbed Wilder, after which he made thirty-nine more films without him.

But it is a curated selection of their masterpieces made together we want to focus on here, and the prescient way in which they predicted the rise of a popular culture utterly enthralled by, captivated by, and even controlled by the insular vagaries of the self-centered spotlight we all now take so much for granted—a world of postmodern culture whose grim consequences we often fail to see. It suddenly occurred to me one day, while off from school and pretending to have the flu but instead watching old classic movies on television as usual, that films were our contemporary cathedral murals, our stained-glass windows. The film that first illuminated the modernist history of art for me was *Sunset Boulevard*, with its arresting opening scene of a dead William Holden floating eerily in a swimming pool, shot from the bottom, looking up.

I was ten years old when I first saw *Sunset Boulevard*, and its impact has never left me, not even over fifty years later. Sometimes I wish it would, or could. *My* relative? He conceived, wrote, and produced this psychotic little psalm? This seemed more like philosophy or sociology assuming the shape of popular entertainment, and doing so in either a comedic or tragic form. And it did it all from within the confines of a claustrophobic and impossibly mismatched creative marriage. The realization that films actually *were* paintings that moved, so to speak, has never entirely left me, and it has also drawn me into a love affair with movies that accepts the fact that they are a stolen series of photographic stills rapidly filtered past a shining lens.

That's what makes them magic in the first place, that and their ability to transport us into alternate realities. But few of the artists toiling in the film inferno of the West Coast would become emblems of such an enigmatic collaboration, one seamlessly merging art with business, quite so vividly as this odd couple, whose movies still have the power to captivate us today. It was called the Golden Age of Hollywood with good reason. Among the many screenwriters, producers, and directors who blazed that ever-expanding trail, few would have quite the lasting impact on both comedy *and* tragedy as impressive and influential as Brackett and Wilder.

They were ironically referred to as the "happiest couple in Hollywood," despite the fact that they disliked each other intensely, and the artistic franchise or "brand" they forged—often identified literally by critics as "brackettandwilder," as if they were one person—permanently places them in the Golden Age pantheon as the makers of *two* kinds of cinema: the screwball comedy and the film noir tragedy. Their cinematic works reveal the paradoxical nature of a peculiar genius: They were mutual muses trapped in a dark mirror of their own making, together. How they accomplished this monumental achievement, and the nature of their often painful collaboration, forms the basis of this book, which seeks to provide a critical joint biography of their partnership.

It's not an account of the individuals themselves so much as of their exotic bonding into a single creative structural unit making movies together, as well as an exploration of the meaning and value of the movies they made. For now, we can all savor the alchemy of their fraught and fight-filled partnership by viewing the remarkable output that resulted from it. Their explosive teamwork touched more hearts and minds than perhaps any other collaboration before or since. Along with Preston Sturges, they were also arguably the first example of the independent-producer phenomenon, now so prevalent in our popular cinematic culture.

Now, of course, it's not as if this remarkable creative partnership didn't get sufficient recognition during their artistic and commercial liaison. After all, an armload of Academy Award nominations for writing, producing, and directing, over the course of some thirteen films made together, and another twenty or so created after their intense breakup and divorce, is certainly acclaim enough for most mortals.

But now might be a good time to cast a glance back at what we loved most, and what we most miss, about the Golden Age of Hollywood and the cast of characters who gave it its luster. Together Brackett and Wilder helped construct the early era of Hollywoodland, an architecturally scaled prescription drug designed to help people survive two world wars, the Great Depression, the Cold War, and many other lesser, daily, but equally unsettling challenges. Naturally, the stormy nature of their working methods together, while being well-known within the Hollywood industry among peers and colleagues, was an utterly unknown element to the audiences they so effectively entertained, and who of course could not have cared less whether they liked or hated each other, as long as they kept the hits coming.

Theirs may not have been the happiest partnership, but it was certainly the most innovative and prolific of the time. Charles Brackett actually helped Billy Wilder *become* Billy Wilder, fighting so hard with him over creative, literary, and production values that eventually Mr. Wilder decided to become a director in order to free himself of the collaborative double-persona that had served them both so well for many successful years.

Their battles were apparently the stuff of legend, in a creative marriage made in hell, scintillatingly brilliant but mostly emotionally unpleasant. Like McCartney and Lennon, another of the most influential artistic partnerships in history (and one most appropriately designated in that order), Charles Brackett and Billy Wilder each needed the balancing and opposite aspect of the other's artistic and emotional temperament in order to most fruitfully manage their mutual gifts. One without the other could be great, compelling, even delightful, but together they formed an almost incomprehensibly brilliant single unit: the head and tail of a superbly minted coin.

As part of a series of profiles of famous cinematic artists for the *New York Times*, Phil Koury shared some insights into Brackett and Wilder's Midas touch in 1948 under the headline "The Happy Union of Brackett and Wilder," which is likely where that other wildly inaccurate tagline—"the happiest couple in Hollywood"— originated. Koury's piece was an effusively praiseworthy item about their unique skill at mastering creative differences to the benefit of both and the advantage of whatever project they were working on at any given time. Their "drastically disparate backgrounds" also some- how formed what Matthew Dessem in The Dissolve described as a "harmonious and productive partnership."

An amazing understatement, considering how often they came to almost killing each other along the way. In his profile, Koury wrote, "It is impossible to tell from a study of one of their scripts, where Wilder ends and Brackett begins." Yet despite this charm- ing mythology, Wilder chose to narrowly characterize their creative dynamic many years later for *The Paris Review*, in 1996: "It's like a box of matches: you pick up the match and strike it against the box, and there's always fire, but then one day there is a small corner of that abrasive paper left for you to strike the match on. It's not there anymore." Perhaps, but which partner was the match and which was the box?

Even before separating, Brackett and Wilder had already begun to work apart, with Billy creating *Double Indemnity* in 1944 on his own (though the original treatment was co-written by both men), while Charles Brackett would receive an Academy Award nomination for Best Motion Picture Story for *To Each His Own* in 1946. Then, after the partnership could no longer sustain the pressures of divergent personalities and stylistic approaches, Brackett would win one Oscar for *Titanic*, in 1953, and be nominated for Best Picture for *The King and I*, in 1956. He then went on to a very active and successful role as a dependable solo producer, delivering *Ten North Frederick* (1958),

Journey to the Center of the Earth (1959), *High Time* (1960), and *State Fair* (1962), among many others.

Wilder was, of course, no slouch either. He would combine talents with I. A. L. Diamond to considerable acclaim on *Some Like It Hot* (1959), *The Apartment* (1960), and *The Fortune Cookie* (1966). He ventured into consistently compelling territory with such films as *Ace in the Hole* (1951), *Stalag 17* (1953), *Witness for the Prosecution* (1957), and on up to *The Front Page* (1974). But despite his frequent victories, even with a few flops, something was missing. According to Andre Soares of Alt Film Guide, although some of Wilder's post-Brackett films were received well, they "generally lacked the subtlety and sophistication found in some of his earlier work with Brackett." I tend to agree.

In 1960, then fully ensconced in his own highly successful, if less masterful, solo production career, Brackett remarked to *Time* magazine that he felt Wilder must have "outgrown his divided fame." This was possibly a discreet way of saying that his former partner had no longer wanted to share the glory jointly and was finally able to accept what he wanted to ambitiously do all along: make it to the top all on his own. For Dessem in The Dissolve, "It clearly wasn't a pleasant topic for either man, and a combination of their reticence and the passage of time had made the answers to many questions about their collaboration murky and obscure. But not completely unanswerable. Luckily for all of us, Brackett, a onetime president of the Academy of Motion Picture Arts and Sciences, had a grandson named Jim Moore who donated 975 folders of scripts, letters, receipts and memos to their archives."

Since Billy Wilder was always ready to talk to anybody at any time about anything, the existing scholarship on him is ample. And since Wilder survived Brackett by over three decades, he was able to craft a mythology of his prominence in the partnership, almost at the expense of his vital collaborator. Indeed, this myth-building of

Wilder's was something he had already ardently commenced even when they were still working together as a team. Brackett was always the more retiring and circumspect of the partners, so the existence of his personal journals, as the place he chose to do most of his talking, is an especially priceless archive.

The diary transcriptions cover the years 1932 through 1949, the great bulk of Brackett's time with Wilder, and they're at the Academy library for anyone to read. I'm probably not alone in lamenting the fact that the autobiography Brackett had at one point considered writing—probably a monumental task of introspection and retrospection, leaving aside the work that his secretary Helen Hernandez would have to do transcribing his cramped handwriting—never did materialize, although at least some of his diaries did eventually get collated and published by Columbia University Press, in a book skillfully edited by Anthony Slide.

Wilder, on the other hand, wrote voluminously, in several memoirs and a boatload of articles, essays, and interviews, almost as if to ensure that the history books contained a version of their soap opera that was most favorable to *him*. Fair enough, I suppose. It was often rough going and presumably a long time both coming and going. Wilder confided to his biographer Charlotte Chandler that working with a co-writer was "more intimate" than a marriage. So when things crashed, they really crashed.

And perhaps the fact that Brackett knew Wilder so well, maybe too well, was at least one of the reasons for wanting his independence from his elder American writing mentor—the one who did, it's best to recall, practically teach him English when he first emigrated from Austria. Wilder further clarified his estimation of partnerships to Chandler like this: "It's like pulling on the end of a rope. If you're going to collaborate with yourself, you don't need a collaborator. You need to have the rope stretched as tautly as you can get it. Out of the friction comes the spark and the sparkle."

Though Brackett and Wilder's partnership eventually devolved into a soap opera itself—a story almost competing with those in *The Lost Weekend* and *Sunset Boulevard*, their two memorable Oscar gems—I am less concerned with that soap opera per se than with the magical way they operated in unison (when they did, of course), and how the symbiosis that Wilder described as both a taut rope and a box of matches actually worked. How on earth did they manage to pull it off, that joyride together into the ranks of Hollywood royalty? And what might the answer to that question, if indeed here is one, tell us all about the inner sanctum of significant otherness in general?

It was from this broiling cauldron of cinematic creativity that some of the most stylistically prophetic and entertaining films ever produced came into being, turning a caustic lens on the dream industry that sustained them both, and predicting the rise of an age of utter self-absorption and celebrity worship—our age. More than seventy years after the curtain was lowered on their somber partnership, it appears that almost everybody, via the internet and its peculiar spawn of social media, is now "Ready for their close-ups." Ours is a weird world in which reality and actuality, news, artifice, and popular entertainment have all been blurred together in a fascinating but threatening manner, not unlike the eerie shadows of *Sunset Boulevard* itself. Perhaps we have all finally come to collectively witness one singularly compelling truth, first observed by the novelist John Updike: "Celebrity is a mask that eats into the face." And the cinema has always been its most cherished dark mirror.

PART ONE

COMEDY

Comedy is tragedy plus time.

DOROTHY PARKER

CHAPTER ONE

COLLISION COURSE

Coming from Away

Being an outsider is the one thing we all have in common.

ALICE HOFFMAN

Film historian Matthew Dessem has written that Charles Brackett and Billy Wilder "may as well have grown up on different planets." And they really did. The trajectory of their travels toward each other and away from their beginnings has all the makings of an improbable origin myth. If a certain dictator of Austrian lineage hadn't taken control of Germany in 1933, Billy Wilder's family might never have had to flee, along with so many other innocents seeking a new life in the new land. And if Charles Brackett hadn't left the lofty enclave of sophisticated and urbane New York to head westward, he may never have arrived at the doorstep of a film studio looking for ways to reinvent itself, or met Wilder, who was also trying to reinvent himself.

Charles William Brackett, the elder member of the famous filmmaking team by fourteen years, was born on November 26, 1892, in the tony enclave of Saratoga Springs, New York, the son of Mary Corliss and Edgar Truman Brackett. His father was a notable Republican senator whose family roots stretched all the way back to the arrival of Richard Brackett to the Massachusetts Bay Colony in 1629, near present-day Springfield. It is thus quite fair to say that he grew up in what he himself would most likely acknowledge was a privileged and genteel atmosphere. He would even admit that it was white, well-heeled, and WASPy, given that he initially studied law at Harvard University, graduating from Williams College in 1915. He graduated just in time to undertake a youthful overseas adventure by joining the Allied Expeditionary Force during World War I, and he was awarded a French Medal of Honor.

In keeping with his own somewhat lofty pedigree, Brackett married Elizabeth Fletcher—who was a descendent of Stephen Hopkins, of the *Mayflower* expedition—on June 2, 1919. They had two daughters, Alexandra (1920–1965) and Elizabeth (1922–1997). He must have been fond of his wife's family, or at least fond enough later on to marry his wife's sister, Lillian Fletcher, after Elizabeth passed away on June 7, 1948, subsequent to a lengthy battle with alcoholism which left her largely something of a recluse. Charles and Lillian would be wed in 1953, and had no children together. The famed gossip columnist Hedda Hopper wrote about their nuptials on December 27 of that year in the *Los Angeles Times* under the catchy headline "Charlie Brackett marries sister of his first wife."

After quickly realizing that he was far more skilled as a writer than as a barrister, he started quite early on to make a name for himself, selling stories to the *Saturday Evening Post, Collier's,* and *Vanity Fair,* and publishing a series of five highly regarded novels: *Counsel of the Ungodly* (1920), *Week-End* (1925), *That Last Infirmity* (1926), *American Colony* (1929), and *Entirely Surrounded* (1930). It was with *American Colony,* in which he chronicled the lives and lifestyles of his fellow expatriates and friends—writers and artists such as F. Scott Fitzgerald, Ernest Hemingway, and Gertrude Stein—that he first came to national attention as a notable narrator of postwar American cultural ideas and social attitudes. Upon taking up residence once again in America, specifically New York, he became the chief drama critic for *The New Yorker* and also continued to publish many stories elsewhere.

Like many lauded writers of the era during the period between the two wars, it seemed inevitable that he too, like so many of his literary friends, would be lured to America's glitzy West Coast, where a massive boom in moviemaking was accelerating so quickly that actual literary figures were needed to fill the demand for perpetual screenplay production. It was to be there, in August 1936, that Brackett would encounter Billy Wilder and enter into the arranged creative marriage unexpectedly fabricated by the matchmaker executives of Paramount Studios. Reflecting in his diary years later upon his first blind dates with Billy, he clearly enunciated what eventually became their primary working method together: "The thing to do was suggest an idea, then have it torn apart and despised. In a few days it would be apt to turn up again, slightly changed, as Wilder's idea. Once I adjusted to that way of working, our lives were much simpler."

Billy Wilder, the ever-industrious Austrian immigrant who made America his home, was born Samuel Wilder (Vilde in German, Shmuel Vildr in Yiddish), on June 22, 1906, to a Polish Jewish family in Sucha Beskidzka, while it was still a part of the fabled Austro-Hungarian Empire. He once described his hometown to his eventual partner Brackett as being half an hour from Vienna, by telegraph. His parents were Eugenia, who gave him the nickname "Billie," and Max Wilder, who ran a small but successful and well-known cake shop in his town's train station. Max had the usual idea of his son (one of two brothers, the other being Lee, who also became a filmmaker) following in the family business. Billy, who changed his name after arriving in America, had other ideas besides selling cakes and took the train instead, to Vienna, where he started to work as a journalist rather than studying at the University of Vienna.

While working as a reporter in 1926, he met and interviewed the renowned jazz band leader Paul Whiteman, whose orchestra was on tour there at the time. Young Wilder, who was a big fan of jazz, impressed the musician so much that he took the ambitious twenty-year-old along with him to Berlin. In that hotbed of avant-garde culture and renegade social mores, Wilder easily and quickly lived and worked among the movers and shakers of the era, while being introduced hither and yon by the generous Whiteman. Wilder was a gregarious socializer, bon vivant, and raconteur even then, climbing the networking and connections ladder in the entertainment field while deciding that writing was to be his ideal vocation. Prior to that decision, however, he also got by as a taxi dancer, a paid partner spending time with customers on a dance-by-dance basis for the length of a single song.

For a time that paid partner profession was even a hot trend in America, where Columbia Pictures made a supposedly risqué film with Barbara Stanwyck in 1931 called *Ten Cents a Dance*. Produced by Lionel Barrymore, of all people, it featured the racy tagline "She was a dance hall hostess, but the band never played 'Home Sweet Home' for her." The socially acceptable format for meeting and greeting total strangers in a semi-intimate setting didn't last long in America, however, though it still persists in some parts of the world. At first it might be difficult to imagine the diminutive Wilder being active in this role, however his huge personality and bubbly energy never presented any obstacles for warmly engaging with the opposite sex, or the same sex, for that matter.

Wilder soon enough left the dance floor for the newspaper and magazine floors of Berlin tabloid publications. He initially wrote crime and sports stories as a stringer, but he also rapidly developed an interest in filmmaking. He had roles as first a screenwriter and then producer on twelve German films, in an early echo of his later professional capacity in America. After Hitler's alarming rise to power,

Wilder decamped to Paris, where he quickly made his directorial debut with *Mauvaise Graine* (French for "Bad Seed") in 1934. By the time that film had its premiere, Wilder had already relocated to Hollywood, leaving behind a family without the means or skills required to fully reinvent themselves as he could. His mother, grandmother, and stepfather were all victims of the Holocaust. Like many other émigrés of that woeful epoch, the existential outcome impacted his temperament and attitudes for the rest of his life.

Pre-Hollywood, however, Wilder's very first film had focused on a wealthy young playboy who somehow becomes embroiled in the activities of local car thieves. Wilder didn't really know what he was doing on set but had such a high degree of confidence and self-mastery that he was easily able to convince others that he did. Having arrived in Paris from Berlin in 1933, he took up residence at Hotel Ansonia, which served as a shelter for members of the German film business who had fled their homeland to escape the threat that soon enveloped a country, a continent, and the entire world. As he later characterized his on-set, in-action apprenticeship to Charlotte Chandler, "I directed out of pure necessity and without any experience. I cannot say I had any fun, there was pressure."

Low budgets demanded that he make creative use of real-life locations as opposed to sets: "The camera was mounted on the back of a truck or in a car. We were constantly improvising. We were doing *nouvelle vague* [new wave] a quarter of a century before they invented a fancy name for it." Even after relocating to Hollywood, "I still didn't think of myself as a director, not exactly. I wasn't certain I liked being a director, but I did know I could do it. That was satisfying." But his days as a Hollywood director were still in the misty future at this early stage. First he had to pay his dues by working in the studio trenches—side by side with Charles Brackett, as it turned out—for a full eight years of writing other people's movies before he could finally establish himself as the director of his own work.

Wilder learned about how to be an American writer from the senior and already extensively published and polished author Brackett, who happily mentored him along in those heady early days, and he learned they could both make highly acclaimed names for themselves as writers for hire. Especially when doing it together. They were, in fact, on a collision course of exquisite proportions.

* * *

A decade before their fateful encounter in the expatriate capital of the world, 1925 must be considered a landmark year for both men as well as a kind of unlikely road map for the events that brought them together in the first place. Brackett had commenced his first flirtation with the dream factory when his short story "Interlocutory," which had appeared in the *Saturday Evening Post* on March 24, 1924, was adapted as a film titled, somewhat less intriguingly, *Tomorrow's Love*. No surviving copies of this film appear to exist. It starred Pat O'Malley and Agnes Ayres in a silent six-reel farce-romance comedy directed by Paul Bern, who ended up being more famous as the husband of Jean Harlow than anything else. In one of Hollywood's most surreal episodes, he committed suicide after their honeymoon, after apologizing for "the frightful wrong I have done you." For our purposes, he is also famous for giving his first taste of the cinema experience to Charles, who went west along with his story to witness its transformation into celluloid.

Tellingly, one newspaper review of the film observed that folks all said these newlyweds were a perfect match, and they were, since every fight ended in a draw. That description could also have been an equally apt characterization for the Brackett and Wilder professional liaison.

1925 was also the year that Wilder had gotten his first job as a writer for the slightly disreputable tabloids *Die Bühne* and *Die Stunde*, and started living the fast life in Berlin at only nineteen years of age. It was a life which he relished, later describing to Charlotte Chandler in a rather ambiguous reference for her profile of him: "Those hot nights when I was screwing girls standing up in doorways, and sometimes, alas, no girls, just doorways." That same year, Brackett, after his first flush of film glamour on the West Coast, was in New York again for the publication of his second novel, *Week-End*, which was so favorably reviewed in *The New Yorker* ("He is said by his intimates to be just like his book, which means that he is slim, sophisticated, young, and sensible to aesthetics, both healthy and slightly off color") that editor Harold Ross hired him as the magazine's drama critic. The remainder of that decade saw him actively reviewing theater plays, writing more novels, and observing from a distance as Hollywood adapted a few more of his crisply written short stories into films, usually in a more florid style.

When Brackett started his stint at *The New Yorker* in September 1927, poor—literally poor—Billy Wilder had woefully taken to the dance floor at the Hotel Eden, successfully making women believe they were his dream dance partner. But he was also writing a series of short stories about his surreal dance escapades and even found time, when not fantasy shuffling, to co-write his first film with Robert Siodmak, *People on Sunday*, which became an unexpected hit and enabled him to talk his way in a new job at UFA, the Universum Film Aktiengeselleschaft, where he rattled off some twelve fresh screenplays in the blink of a wrist. Though each not yet encountering the other, the literary orbit of the two future partners was circling ever closer to doing so, as it does in many of the obvious cases of synchronicity (as Dr. Jung called it), or meaningful coincidence, that we've witnessed in the course of our circuitous narrative.

As Wilder explained to biographer Chandler, his experience as a UFA filmmaker, a Berliner, and an expatriate artist, and his sources of most future inspiration were fairly basic: "We all got our ideas about Hollywood from the Hollywood movies. We believed what we saw. Hollywood represented America for us, unimaginable. I remember a scene in a Hollywood film I saw in Berlin. A tramp comes up to a man who just got out of a limousine and he asks him for the time. The rich man reaches into his pocket and takes out this great gold pocket watch, and he gives it to him. For me, that was America." And how many of us still derive our concepts of America directly from the mythologies crafted by the dream merchants of Hollywood, rather than from actual historical study? Chandler's comment about his origins and flight path reveal something of his displacement in time and space: "All of Billy Wilder's memories before the age of twenty-six were in German. After that, except for a year in Paris, he lived his life in English."

His dreams, of course, were on celluloid. Film scholar Gerd Gemünden astutely discusses "the illusionary dimension of filmmaking" in his *Continental Strangers: German Exile Cinema, 1933–1951*, writing, "even when in the service of entertainment, impersonation and masquerade always entail a political dimension, serving as allegory for the price the exile has to pay in his quest for assimilation, for blending in, or for mere survival." Gemünden has also noted how prominent the shifting of identity is in Wilder's work in general. Such complexity of identity is quite understandable considering the exile's real-life role as a person who has been, to use Arnold Schoenberg's phrase, "driven into paradise."

Further, what Joseph McBride identifies as the dilemma of Jewish identify in Hollywood is made all the more convoluted as a result of sharing the exile status with those who came before them: "Although Hollywood was enriched with the exiles' presence, many immigrant Jews felt they were treated like second-class citizens and aliens not only by average Americans but even by some of their fellow Jews in the studios."

In 1933, when Wilder was escaping Berlin by the skin of his teeth, Brackett was summoned west by the mighty RKO Studios, where the mercurial David Selznick assigned him to adapt an article by Adela Rogers St. Johns into a screenplay. Perhaps having a bad day, or missing his usual breakfast of amphetamines, Selznick was not impressed by Brackett's very brief film story conference and he was summarily dispatched to New York, which suited him just fine.

Meanwhile, early on in his émigré tenure, Wilder ably demonstrated the first of his many instances of good fortune by getting one of the screenplays, *Pam-Pam*, which he had adapted from stories he'd originally submitted to his German UFA bosses, accepted by Columbia Pictures. The truly remarkable part of his rise in the business of penning American film stories at this stage was the amazing fact that he spoke only German and French.

Columbia kept Wilder on a nominal salary for a short-term contract of a couple of months—certainly enough to prevent him ever having to return to the dance floor—during which, astonishingly enough, he actually worked with a translator to write his script. Subsequently, without a job, he had to leave America again until he got his residency permit. He did receive it, after hanging about in Mexicali for a while, and managed to resume his slow-motion rise to fame and glory, at least in his own vivid imagination. All Brackett had to do was to shift his attention back to New York, his principal stomping grounds, and hang out with his illustrious literary and theater friends in the legendary Algonquin. But whether it was creative visualization on Wilder's part, or the swanky good fortune seemingly fueling Brackett's own parallel ascent, chance brought them back into its embrace in 1936, again in Hollywood, through the good graces of Paramount Studios.

But as we all remember from those memorable lines from the sparkling comedy *Flying Down to Rio*, spoken repeatedly to Fred Astaire by an Italian gigolo trying to justify his unlikely love affair, "Chance is the fool's name for fate." And so it was for Brackett and Wilder, a former gigolo (of sorts) and a senator's son, and both gifted writers, each in their own unique and idiosyncratic way, who would be swept up into the lusty arms of a dream factory always on the hunt for fresh content. They were both just about ready to jump on board the fast-moving Hollywood train and never look back.

Whereas Wilder was known to be a prolific talker, one capable of granting interviews to parking meters and still revealing a wealth of valuable insights, Brackett was the more taciturn raconteur who shared his intimate feelings only privately with his diary, almost as if he were interviewing himself. But it is in these two spheres, the public and the private, where the partners both laid bare their perspectives on their professional and personal lives. Indeed, Billy's enthusiasm for talking, even in his fractured Viennese accent, often prompted him to divulge something more like a journal entry, but in real time. For Wilder, an interview actually *was* a form of diary, while for Brackett, his diary entries were a kind of conversation with himself.

One of the best sources for interview insights from Wilder must surely be the book edited by Robert Horton called *Billy Wilder: Interviews*, in which he is often as unbridled as if he were at home sipping a drink and jotting down musings. A good example being how forthright he was to *Playboy* in sharing a persistent feeling that he carried with him everywhere, what he glumly called "the story of my life." Wilder, seemingly out of nowhere, started to reminisce in the most mournful manner, unbidden, describing his hand-to-mouth existence in a Berlin rooming house during the difficult period in which he was trying to break into filmmaking. His own room was next to the house's communal bathroom, with a broken toilet that dripped all night long, keeping him up, even seeping into his dreams. To counteract his misery, Wilder would use his prodigious imagination to conjure up a lovely waterfall in nature.

Twenty-five years later, once he had actually *become* Billy, super-successful and über-famous, he was indulging himself at a swank spa in Austria, a marvelous location that boasted a beautiful waterfall among its many opulent splendors. "There I am in bed," Wilder remembered, "listening to the waterfall. And after all I have been through, all the trouble and the money I've made, all the awards and everything else, there I am in that resort, and all I can think of is that goddamned toilet. That . . . is the story of my life." Few things could encapsulate the enigma that is Billy Wilder more than that memory shared with an unsuspecting magazine interviewer. It was also the secret prescription that helped him survive: never forgetting the experience of almost not surviving.

Horton's own observations are also quite salient on the subject of disclosure: "Wilder's voice in interviews is finally the same as his voice in his films. His war movies are comedies, his romances contain suicide attempts. He has made film classics narrated by the dead and the dying, he showers satirical darts on conventional heroes." Meanwhile, Brackett's sort of sharing is entirely evident from his very first diary entry, made in 1932, still four years away from being anointed as Wilder's mentor-partner: "The University Club, New York City. Impelled to write a diary by my pleasure in reading the diaries kept by my great Uncle William Corliss through the Civil War Years." Little did he know that he was about to embark upon his own personal civil war for a dozen years with his hard-edged émigré mentee.

Brackett was also able to share, since no one would ever read these musings, or so he thought, some of the day-to-day tribulations that dogged his private life, as on June 26 while traveling from Saratoga to Stockbridge to spend the day with his wife Elizabeth at a psychiatric facility there: "Recuperating from a sad and trying winter. En route I meditated on the advantages of have so good-tempered and non-domineering a wife." By September, he is quietly heralding his arrival in Hollywood: "California was a long sage-green valley. We landed at Los Angeles." He met the director of a film he was assigned to, George Cukor, and was then first exposed to the odd vagaries of the screenwriting craft.

And by October, he is already weary: "I have thought sadly today of my two stupidities: the fact that I am unable to realize the smallness of my accomplishment and the fact that I have very little sense of the passage of time. It has been months since I have had anything published." Remorse—a little inexplicable considering all the stories, novels, plays, and scripts he had already created—appeared to stalk him early on, with November bringing with it a doldrum-like dirge: "As I write, I am just about passing into my 40th year, and I am as discouraged about my career as one can be who is cursed with a sanguine disposition. I have an interesting, scattered life, and I have gotten nowhere. I wish I had the answer." Paradoxically, one answer awaited him in the feverishly gifted brain of Billy Wilder. But he might still need some convincing, since by 1933 he was already burdened by the core nature of Hollywood, "That, in Hollywood, I should have thought the most tedious thing tolerable is a commentary on Hollywood." Brackett was obviously already casting a jaundiced gaze on a dream domain he would return to castigating, albeit much more entertainingly, fifteen years later.

He had been actively working on Hollywood scripts as a staff writer since 1932, when he was working on *Little Women* for George Cukor, among other projects. That was the year he also started making diary entries, covering everything from what projects he was working on with whom to what he was eating for lunch. Perhaps he even imagined that one day they might prove useful for a book about Hollywood. After his initial disappointing stint out west, the studios called him back again in 1936, putting him into the role of executive writer, a fancy way of saying "hang around until we give you something to do, at a moment's notice." He arrived by train on January 5 and on the next day he optimistically reported for duty. "Called at the office of the head of the Story Dept. to learn that there is no assignment for me, won't be for a couple of days. But am I under salary, my incredulous nerves cry. I don't ask the question."

He also described what he called a hideous day waiting for the anticipated bad reviews for a film on which he wasn't proud of his writing contribution, 1935's *Rose of the Rancho*. "All my leave of absence has been haunted by a dread of the reviews. *The Hollywood Reporter* carried a sullenly disagreeable one. All the composure and perspective I acquired in the East collapsed like foam. Though basically in agreement with the reviews, I resented them hotly. May God give me the strength never to accept a really silly project again." Luckily for him, some of the silly projects he would be offered also happened to turn out to be masterpieces.

He had been partnered initially with a fellow writer, Frank Partos, who was agreeable enough, if not inspiring, and they were invited to the story department on July 6, where the studio "dangled before us the possibility of working on the next Lubitsch picture, a two week trial thing which I would have refused had Frank not been so anxious for the chance. I don't really know Lubitsch and he makes me uncomfortable. I went to the studio prepared to give a grouchy proposal refusal to shift me to another story. Learned that the other story is *Bluebeard's Eighth Wife*, with Claudette Colbert, with Lubitsch directing. I'm to be teamed with a young Austrian I've seen about for a year or two."

Brackett was suddenly conscripted and pressed into service by Manny Wolf, the story editor head of Paramount's writer's department. Wolf had called Brackett in to his office one day to make a formal introduction: "Charlie Brackett, meet Billy Wilder. From now on, you're a team." Cue the fireworks. Though I have no firsthand or direct evidence of this notion, my reading of Wilder's ambitions is such that I feel strongly that his initial internal response was something along the lines of: Fine, I'll work with this American guy for a couple of pictures, learn some English, win some Oscars, and then ditch him to go ahead on my own, as a solo act.

For biographer Chandler, Wilder's new partner had just what he needed to make a serious go of it in a domain still somewhat unfamiliar to him: a unique Yankee sensibility. He had what she generously referred to as "The Brackett Touch," gently echoing the stylistic identifier previously bestowed on the first big-time director they worked for in Hollywood, Ernst Lubitsch. That touch, in the estimation of many who encountered or worked with Billy, provided just the kind of active *opponent* he needed. Billy saw this instantly as well, and he patiently allowed it to sink into his own overall ethos: "Brackett was sort of a country gentleman, with political beliefs to the right of Herbert Hoover. I was for Roosevelt and the New Deal. Brackett and I didn't think the same way at all, but it's this difference of opinions that makes for a good collaboration." Up to a point, of course: "Sometimes we would argue violently, but that was good. That was how we got along. Brackett forced me to *think* in English, especially when I argued with him, which was a lot."

Lubitsch, their first directorial boss, knew Wilder's work from Germany and thought the two writers might gel as collaborators. In some annotations Brackett added to his typed diary transcription about the encounter, he described Wilder as a thirty-two-year-old newcomer, "a slim young fellow with a merry face, particularly the upper half of it, the lower half of his face had other implications . . . the face of a naughty cupid . . . Before we were joined in collaboration, I'd known him as a jaunty young foreigner who worked on the fourth floor at Paramount, where I worked."

For the peripatetic Wilder, coming from the near-indigence of tabloid writing, dancing in Berlin doorways, and then living in exile in Paris, he must have felt as if he had landed in the lap of luxury in Los Angeles. And in a way, he had. With the Great Depression still lingering, he had been put on more permanent contract with

Paramount for the princely sum of $250 a week. The studio system was grueling, not least because he still barely spoke English and needed translators to help him out, but it was also the custom to maintain a stable of writers as if they were racehorses waiting to be ridden. After awarding them the boon of a project, the executives required them to hand in material weekly, and if they had no crumbs to offer they'd be rented out to other studios, with the borrowing company paying the salary plus a fee.

Brackett, a much more seasoned author, was earning $1,000 a week with Paramount, although he was rented out to MGM and toiled on aimless projects with Partos, who was an incompatible writing partner. Fired from MGM, he expressed considerable ambivalence about the whole business, stating that though he loathed his assignment it still offended him to be dismissed. Prior to teaming up, both Brackett and Wilder appeared to be on shaky ground in the coldhearted fish-canning business known as film production in the late '30s. It came to pass that they would each work with yet another incompatible writing partner, but this time that fact didn't get in the way of their clicking instantaneously on the creative side of things.

While both were happy to have consistent work, Wilder was especially grateful for the generous guidance provided by the older and more experienced writer—at least at first. Wilder biographer Maurice Zolotow has stated that working with Brackett was fruitful because he "was a piece of American literature." And Wilder readily admitted that "Brackett really knew English. He wasn't just an American, he was educated and articulate. He was patient, and he never laughed when I made a mistake in English, which was most of the time. He understood what I meant, and he showed me the right way." Indeed, both men understood exactly what the other meant—where they were coming from, so to speak, not to mention where they both wanted to go. And they put their obvious shared simpatico vibe to good use immediately.

In terms of Wilder's cultural heritage, his transformative new role in Hollywood, and his vulnerable character armor, possibly resulting from his proximity to the infernal occurrences in his homeland, I spoke with the former Director of Programming for the Jewish Film Festival in Toronto, Shlomo Schwartzberg. In our discussion, his aerial take on what made cinema's "Golden Age" shine with such a Euro-vibe was especially insightful regarding the upcoming partnership that would characterize it most vividly:

> The Golden Age of cinema was marked by films that were adult, challenging, and intelligent, with movies that presumed that their potential audiences actually had brains. In the context of the upcoming historical period in which Brackett and Wilder were eventually teamed up by Paramount, roughly 1938 to 1950, the films they wrote, produced, and eventually also directed are considered classics today with good reason: they had snappy dialogue, strong characterization, both male and female, and were directed with verve and style. Once freed of the shackles of censorship (The Hays Code) they also even broke taboos of subject matter, and offered up less glamorous, 'ordinary-looking' movie stars, with identifiably ethnic (Italian, Jewish) characters.
>
> These filmmakers made provocative statements about life as it was actually lived in America. Their movies were not cut from the same cookie cutter. Once they got rolling together, their films were sophisticated, adult, and jaundiced, but not cynical, and they were about how people behave. Most importantly, whether in the comedy or noir domains, they were also highly entertaining and supremely witty. In the early days of their partnership, their temperaments practically melted into each other almost seamlessly, or so it appeared from the outside. Wilder's European background didn't slot him into any limiting boxes creatively, and Brackett's suave Yankee ingenuity blended ideally with the younger writer's daring aplomb.

They both felt they could try to do anything they wanted to in films. The result was a rather superb flexibility that permitted them to take risks, both in the comedic and dramatic realms. Screwball comedy is fast-moving and fast-speaking, off-kilter and not at all predictable in its take on what makes humor function in the real world. Film noirs are dark takes on the human condition whose characters, predominantly women, behave extremely badly and no one is who they appear to be on the surface. It's still something of a mystery how this team could excel at both stylistic disciplines. It's equally hard to define or explain the dynamics of two cooperating collaborators whose temperaments are so different that they don't like each other at all, but they still have a magical meshing at play when working together. Creative collaboration can often gel marvelously, even if its practitioners differ so greatly from each other."

Wilder had a certain blasé attitude that appealed to Brackett and "a kind of humor that sparks with mine." I can't help noticing two things about their enforced union in this regard: Brackett's use of the word "spark," which evoked Wilder's own description of what a writer needs in a partner, and also the fact that, in an odd echo of Wilder's recent livelihood in Berlin, they were both being well paid by Paramount to serve as dance partners for each other.

In the early stages, this arrangement proceeded smoothly, with each man taking turns to lead or follow, as all the best dance teams do. But before long, their respective tendencies—Wilder to be gregarious, outgoing, and demonstrative; Brackett to be reticent, retiring, and genteel—rapidly came to the fore in obvious and foreseeable ways. Always willing to be interviewed by almost anybody, anytime, as if to guarantee the personal plotline that he preferred, Billy was active in promoting not just the films they wrote together, but also himself as a progenitor, or at least the charge-leading enthusiast, a pattern that would continue and increase as they shifted inevitably from writing screenplays for other producers, then writing for projects written together and produced by Brackett, to films written together, produced by Brackett and directed by Wilder.

Brackett, meanwhile, was far more comfortable writing in his private diaries, obsessively documenting practically every occurrence, some notable and historic, some minute and quotidian. Luckily for us, these have proved to be a veritable goldmine as a counterpoint to Wilder's public tap-dancing routine. Charlie's grandson Jim Moore was a scrupulous archivist of his grandfather's crimped jottings, realizing that they might one day prove to be a source of historical insights into a volatile yet productive relationship. And indeed they have been, as he points out poignantly in his tender foreword to the compilation edited by Anthony Slide: "Billy Wilder outlived my grandfather by thirty-three years and when my mother and I were discussing working the diaries into a book, she worried that the entries about Billy were too raw to publish in the glow of living legend."

Brackett's diaries illustrate how much of the Wilder "living legend" was in fact constructed by Billy himself, especially once he became versatile enough in the English language to broadcast far and wide a careful narrative designed to place himself in the most favorable, and usually most prominent, light. For Moore, "The diaries make it indisputably clear that the partnership was a solidly professional arrangement based on each writer's unique literary and theatrical skills and bonded in the heat of a very dynamic and unforgiving business. Neither man served at the will of the other. . . . Brackett and Wilder loved each other, hated each other, defended each other, sold each other out, delighted in the partnership, and longed for the pairing to die."

It would of course take thirteen long years for it to die, often in excruciatingly slow motion. I definitely look forward to the family memoir about his grandfather that Moore has intimated he is writing, one from the vantage point of a closely situated insider, as it should shine a bright light on the impact of a crass industry upon sensitive souls such as Charlie.

As difficult as he could often be, one of the many things that Wilder intuitively knew was the necessary number of irritants required for them to function as oysters in the making of pearls. Their output also bears out just how vividly he perceived the immediate chemical reaction that occurred when he first met his future partner. The fact that they were so drastically different was simply the price that both men were willing to pay in the service of their gifts.

In 1945, at the height of their commercial success, critical awards, and fame, and just before things went south, *Liberty* magazine would profile them perfectly, pointing out that Mr. Brackett's poison was Mr. Wilder's meat. The article aptly described how Brackett was distinguished and dapper, resembling the vice president of a small-town bank, whereas Wilder resembled one of the cynical and grubby reporters from the movie *The Front Page*. Years later, Wilder would slyly confirm the obvious to Cameron Crowe by declaring that the only thing they ever had in common was "good writing."

CHAPTER TWO

SHIFTING GEARS

Clutching Down

In Hollywood, we always acquire the finest novels, in order to smell the leather bindings.

ERNST LUBITSCH

The term "double solitaire" refers to a competitive version of the well-known "Klondike" solo card game, in which each player has their own fifty-two-card deck, each with a different backing to distinguish them. The game commences with the player having the lower card on their stack starting. You are required to move cards around only on your own layout, and your turn ends when you are not able to make any more moves. You then turn over the top-facing card on your stack and place it on your opponent's discard pile, at which point their turn commences. An alternative method to taking turns is to play the game as a race, with both opponents moving simultaneously. It has long seemed to me that Brackett and Wilder made their movies by alternating who was in charge at any given time during a joint project, but they also frequently competed with each other to determine who was top dog in the end. This approach— playing sometimes apart, sometimes together—served them effectively throughout their shared careers.

For Jim Sinclair, former executive director of the Cinematheque in Vancouver, British Columbia, "Clearly both were excellent storytellers, both excellent screenwriters in their own rights. But, perhaps as collaborators, Wilder wielded the camera, or the visual tools of cinema, and Brackett wielded the pen—and some kind of special alchemy definitely happened. . . . Their ability to work together collaboratively, despite drastic differences in temperament, that remains a big mystery."

Brackett and Wilder's very first collaborative dream venture has to be considered the height of serendipity, consisting as it did of an unsolicited assignment to write the screenplay for one of Europe's most notable expatriate film directors. Ernst Lubitsch (1892–1947) was a German-born American filmmaker, producer, writer, and actor whose urbane comedies of manners forged a solid reputation for him as Hollywood's most elegant and sophisticated cinema artist. Born the same year as Brackett and coming from the same Teutonic roots as Wilder, he may have felt an affinity for both of these sparkling new writers. Their snappy literary style definitely proved perfect for his own understated visual acumen.

From January through March 1937, Brackett was working on *Bluebeard's Eighth Wife*, mostly at Lubitsch's home, possibly in order to have the fussy director's dissatisfaction more readily available to him. When he did venture out of the office with Billy—for a dinner with his former writing partner Frank Partos and another screenwriter, Irwin Gelsey, for instance—Brackett was often called upon to serve as a referee. On one occasion, "Billy got a little fresh and I had to smack him down, which I was able to do with the authority of complete boredom." Ennui would turn out to be one of Brackett's chief survival mechanisms for thriving work-wise with the voluble Wilder. This proved to be a useful technique, especially when the studio was always interrupting their work on the Lubitsch film by assigning them duties on other movies, such as simultaneously writing a scene for Dorothy Lamour in *The Big Broadcast*—which, as basic literary drones toiling in the typewriter trenches, they were obliged to accept with a grin. It was tough going, though, prompting Brackett to confide that Billy was often "surly" in the office, describing one day in late December as a "fruitless day. Billy is playing young genius—my nerves are on edge." But both Billy and Ernst Lubitsch had other reasons of their own for being out of sorts: the downfall in March 1938 of their beloved homeland, Austria.

Lubitsch was born in Berlin to Simon Lubitsch and Anna Lindenstadt, into a family of Ashkenazi Jews that originally hailed from the portion of the Russian empire now known as Belarus. Like Wilder, he had turned his back on his disappointed father's business, tailoring, to pursue his first love, theater, and by 1911 the young man was already a member of Max Reinhardt's Deutsches Theatre. Though he made his film debut as an actor, in 1913's *The Ideal Husband*, he early on expressed an interest in production and directing. (His last film role would be in the 1920 drama *Sumrun*, which he also directed, opposite the great Pola Negri and Paul Wegener. His early acclaim inspired him to create his own production company and he made his first abortive attempt to go to America in 1921, where the still-stinging aftermath of World War I did not at first provide a welcoming environment. He eventually left Europe for good at the behest of Mary Pickford, a star too huge to care about public sentiment, to direct her in *Rosita*, a 1923 film that became both a critical and commercial success.

He became a free agent after clashing with Pickford and settled in America to commence a string of stylish and sophisticated comedies for Warner Brothers with *The Marriage Circle* (1924), *Lady Windemere's Fan* (1925), and *So This Is Paris* (1926). Subsequently his contract was bought out by Paramount, and he made *The Patriot* for that studio in 1928, which earned him his first Academy Award nomination for Best Director. A string of musical comedies followed, all popular with the public and critics alike, and his first big hit was the sound film *Trouble in Paradise* (1932), which was so ribald that it could only have been made just prior to the reign of Hollywood's stringent moral production code, and in fact was totally withdrawn from circulation after 1935 until 1968.

Writing of the director in the *Los Angeles Times* for a centenary profile, critic Michael Wilmington captured some of what made Lubitsch special: "At once elegant and ribald, sophisticated and earth, urbane and bemused, frivolous yet profound. A man who was amused by sex rather than frightened of it, and who taught a whole culture to be amused by it as well." That puzzling combination of opposed qualities also described his two newest writers, Brackett and Wilder.

Film historian Richard Koszarski shared that same appreciation for Lubitsch and his "touch" in his book *Hollywood Directors, 1914–1940*, calling him "perhaps the most successful of all the talent imported by Hollywood. One major reason for the ease of Lubitsch's transition from Germany to America, and from silents to sound, was the carefully programmed way he approached the production of his films, creating a blueprint for a film that was followed on the set with the precision of a great master craftsman."

His sense of order and control led Paramount to appoint him its overall production manager in 1935, making him the first Hollywood director to also run a significantly large studio operation, producing his own films as well as supervising the creation of films by other directors at the same time. He did, however, have difficulty with the tricky art of delegating authority and sharing in decision-making with others, a talent that would have been essential for managing the production of over sixty films at a time. Paramount released him from that senior oversight position after only a single tempestuous year, freeing him to concentrate solely on his own work.

In 1936, the same year Paramount was pairing the untried team of Brackett and Wilder, Lubitsch became a naturalized citizen of the United States, and would inherit the two assigned screenwriters for their first big break on his upcoming film, the ominously titled *Bluebeard's Eighth Wife*. The trio hit it off, generating an energy that would carry them forward creatively to the making of their first true masterpiece together, *Ninotchka*.

Pretty much at the inception of their collaboration there were clashes aplenty. By February 1939, however, they would be turning out such finessed screenwriting, with *Ninotchka* being perhaps the best early example, that they were already becoming identified as a star—though arguably star-crossed—team. But not without drawbacks, setbacks, and fallbacks, often on overlapping projects, as when Brackett confided to his diary in February that "Billy and I finished the *Ninotchka* script . . . went, in separate cars, to the preview of *Midnight*, it went miraculously well . . . at the office at nine, Billy arrived a few minutes later with a small Bulgarian flute which he played all day. . . . I took it and smashed it across my knee. Billy's face turned scarlet, he rushed from the room and came back in a very bitter mood."

By May, things were going further sideways: "Long day at the office, Billy thought he had a tumor of the brain and spent the afternoon being x-rayed. Worried about Billy's nervous breakdown, which seems to be serious. He plans a trip away for a couple of weeks." Then, on July 27: "Day at the studio trying to work on *Ninotchka*. Violent quarrels with Billy . . . from whom I fear I shall have to part company, much as the thought of working alone now terrifies me, but I doubt the value of any reconciliation with him." Regardless of all the obstacles, however, they pressed on, beginning discussions about scripting a future story for Mitchell Leisen, which would eventually become *Hold Back the Dawn*, for a September 1941 release.

*   *   *

This glimpse into the geography of the imagination triggers one of our most puzzling cultural questions: Why is it that much of our great art, music, films, and literature is so often produced collaboratively by creative partners who can't stand the sight of each other? With Brackett and Wilder being the most apt cinematic example, why do some of the most inventive partnerships involve individuals who can barely be in the same room together, even though they seem to share only one creative soul between them and thus grudgingly acknowledge their reluctant codependence?

Especially if their partnership is one that is collectively celebrated by a wide popular audience that perpetually rewards them for their shared struggle—by bestowing Academy Awards for their movies, for example—their angst still remains acute. One needs to look to the basic foundational level at which point all of these different sets of creative partners intersect, along with all the shared compulsions they have in common: from the intuitive obsessions of a film director like Alfred Hitchcock, caught between control freak David Selznick and his primary musical muse, composer Bernard Herrmann, to the split-screen comedy-tragedy of Brackett and Wilder, feuding while still creating great cinema out of private conflicts. This complex balancing act between such mutual muses also provides a way of separating creative myth from actual artistic practice, of disentangling the popular image of the partners from the actual lives of the players, and most importantly, of appreciating what Shari Benstock has called "the uniquely singular achievements within the collaborative process itself."

Yet despite the perpetually shaky foundations of their teamwork, from the moment their partnership commenced, under the frequently shifting gaze of their new directorial boss, it was still instantly clear that the two mercurial writers managed to craft great screenplays together. Without getting along very well or liking each other, each still respected the other's strengths and tolerated any weaknesses. Even though they were like oil and water, they still somehow managed to manufacture an ideal sort of salad dressing in the script, which, when sprinkled over Lubitsch's images and action, almost made him smile. Wilder's gift for structure and Brackett's for dialogue were both essential ingredients in the mix. As Brackett noted in an early and revealing assessment of his new colleague, "He is a hard, conscientious worker, without a very sensitive ear for dialogue, but a beautiful constructionist. He has a passion for the official joke of a second-rate dialogist."

Both men were jealous of Lubitsch's affection. In one instance, Wilder picked a fight after the director seemed to favor Brackett, shouting, "You and he will be making a baby together before this picture is through." And Brackett was conscious of the fact that Lubitsch and Wilder shared a culture and language. One day at Lubitsch's house, Brackett noticed the two men were even wearing the same outfit, gray trousers and maroon sweatshirts: "It was a very dreamlike effect."

The slightly rumpled yet suave and charmingly cheeky Lubitsch's famed "touch" is light and bright in 1938's *Bluebeard's Eighth Wife*. A battle-of-the-sexes farce set on the French Riviera, the film has Gary Cooper (slightly miscast; maybe Cary Grant was booked up) as an American millionaire whose seven marriages have all ended in divorce—and with hefty settlements, for him. He is determined to make Claudette Colbert, daughter of a penniless French marquis (Edward Everett Horton, perfectly cast) his imagined wealthy wife number eight. She's just as determined to avoid his advances, and the fate of his previous seven spouses, resorting to drastic measures, even after she agrees to marry him, to maintain an upper hand in a situation that will quickly get out of control.

James Harvey, author of *Romantic Comedy in Hollywood*, calls *Bluebeard's Eighth Wife* "a comedy of the delayed fuck"—one in a long

line of films in that unique genre. David Niven has an early supporting role, more or less playing David Niven, while Cooper and Colbert
were two of Paramount's biggest studio stable stars at the time. Gloria
Swanson, of later *Sunset Boulevard* fame, had played in a 1923 silent
version of the same story, directed by Sam Wood and based on Alfred
Savoir's original 1921 play, *La Huitième Femme de Barbe-Bleue*. The
film went on to become the twenty-first highest-grossing movie of
1938, despite the observation of many that Cooper was slightly out of
step and the script was often bright and spritely but also illogical and
fragile. Of course, that's what made it a screwball comedy.

The response to *Bluebeard*, both then and now, has always been
somewhat mixed and muted, to say the least. A timely take was
provided by Frank Nugent in the *New York Times* review of 1938,
headlined "Cooper Comes a Cropper": "Ernst Lubitsch has slipped
the boxing gloves over his brass knuckles again and is tapping out
a few more Lubitsch touches. Although not a bad comedy by our
depressed standards, it has the dickens of a time trying to pass off
Gary Cooper as a multi-marrying millionaire. It all ends in an asy-
lum, with Bluebeard in a straitjacket, which proves they're always
getting the wrong man: the one they should have grabbed was the
chap who picked Mr. Cooper for the part." Luckily, the leading man
for their follow-up film would be everyone's idea of perfect casting,
the debonair and understated Melvyn Douglas.

Rachel Bellwoar has written on Comicon.com that "the verdict
you're going to consistently encounter with *Bluebeard's Eighth Wife*
is that it is one of Ernst Lubitsch's lesser films. How seriously to take
'lesser' when it's being used to refer to Lubitsch is something to keep
in mind but one of the main criticisms thrown at the picture is that
it's misogynistic. But *Bluebeard's Eighth Wife* isn't just for Lubitsch
completists."

Personally I think that the misogynistic label is an unfair one,
and only looms large in retrospect given how much the times have

changed since that period in social history—although the film's ending in a mental institution is certainly a bit touchy. Any anti-woman sentiment was, I believe, quite unintentional, and more the result of adapting a farcical storyline from a theater setting during a time when the two screenwriters were just getting to know the ins and outs of working together.

At this point, Brackett and Wilder were not yet entirely thought of as a unit. That perception would come more fully into focus only after their follow-up effort for Lubitsch, who was happy with their pairing and the results, since *Bluebeard's Eighth Wife* made money and, while not exactly a great work of art (that would happen with *Ninotchka*), was still an enjoyable piece of studio entertainment. Paramount also found ways to make use of them, or try to, separately as well, with Brackett finding out in 1938 that Wilder was apparently working solo on a script. He wrote, with typical arch humor, that he was "delighted at a respite from Billy and will work hard to see, if I'm a good boy, if it can't be made permanent." It couldn't, and it didn't.

"Garbo Laughs!" proclaimed the adverts for 1939's *Ninotchka*, which featured the usually austerely serious Greta Garbo in her very first comedy. "Stalin won't like it!" observed a contemporary *New York Times* review. Another effervescent exemplar of the Lubitsch touch, this political satire and romantic comedy, penned by the now-crack writing team, has Garbo as a stern Soviet commissar newly arrived in decadent capitalist Paris. She's there to rein in a troika of bumbling Bolshevik comrades—including Bela Lugosi—who are trying to sell some state-confiscated jewels but who have instead become seduced by capitalist luxuries unheard of by them before their assignment. Icy Ninotchka soon finds herself melting herself under capitalism's charms—and those of Leon, a debonair French count played by Melvyn Douglas, who sets out on his own assignment, to woo Greta's cool character. The scene where Douglas finally gets Garbo to crack up remains a high point of Hollywood romantic comedy to this day.

This suave and appealing comedy, made when Europe was teetering on the brink of war, is also not without its darker, cynical undertones, often taking swipes at Soviet tyranny, Tsarist-era corruption, and the emerging Nazi menace. Joshua Rothkopf of *Time Out New York* extols a few of its virtues enthusiastically: "*Ninotchka* is delicate flirtation and political satire made into a perfect whole, a reminder of perfect skills that studio writers today have largely forgotten about or lost touch with." One of my favorite claims by any director ever was made by Lubitsch himself, who observed that "I've been to Paris France. And I have been to Paris Paramount. Paris Paramount is much better."

Ninotchka was Brackett and Wilder's second attempt at writing in tandem, and their first massively magical and award-winning hit, but it is important to remember that it was a script originally devised by Walter Reisch but rejected by Lubitsch, who called in the wunderkind unit to completely renovate and resuscitate the text. This they managed to do swiftly and almost supernaturally (it took only about a month), transforming the wild storyline into pure gold, proving again that for many viewers Brackett and Wilder were the gloves that Lubitsch wore in order to most effectively transmit that famous touch. Every moment of this satirical romp, one which also contains some heavy-duty social and political commentary cleverly masked by the mayhem, is sheer genius. Audiences adored it and made it a huge hit commercially. Critics and historians seemed to sense right away that something significant artistically had been achieved, with Iris Barry asking for the script to be submitted to the then still-new film library in the Museum of Modern Art in New York, commenting that she was "absolutely certain that it must be one of the most dazzling film scripts ever conceived."

For their rapid and intuitive turnaround, Brackett and Wilder received their first Academy Award nomination, which they shared with Walter Reisch. Unfortunately, 1939 was also the award season for a little movie called *Gone with the Wind*, for which Sidney Howard won for Best Screenplay. Nonetheless, most historians agree that it was from this moment onward that Hollywood began to identify them, together, in print, as the integrated structural unit of "brackettandwilder." Despite how cozy that epithet sounds, however, their working method was anything but. Wilder was commonly seen stomping around their shared office waving and whacking his riding crop, a gesture that both mystified and sometimes unnerved the more sedate Brackett.

Charlie would take in hand the actual physical act of writing, in longhand, during their blistering sessions, jotting out their scripts on yellow legal pads, a distant echo of his Harvard Law days, and passing them off to their secretary, Helen Hernandez. (Hers are in fact the diaries I tend to wish had been collected and published.) Their energetic exchanges also extended far beyond the entirely professional realm, and though they were by no means friends, Brackett finding Wilder's habit of showing off in front of women off-putting to say the least: "a horrible mauley, hand kissing quality which is really nauseating." Charlie was often called upon to help Billy with his domestic life as well, as a kind of referee in his fights with wife Judith.

The writing pair developed, over time, a kind of passive-aggressive technique common to many artistic partnerships. Wilder seemed to find it difficult to work if he had been praised, perhaps a nod to his fondness for combative approaches, so they tended to schedule meetings with executives in the late afternoon. Another strategy, since they were very sensitive to judgments in general, and the bosses had a habit of changing their writing as if they knew what they were doing, was to write as long into the night as possible, in order to discourage any rewriting of their material in the face of tight studio deadlines. And this is the boiling creative cauldron, the hotly contested territorial division, out of which Brackett and Wilder managed, against all odds, to pull off the supreme coup of their shared screenplays, and later on, the disciplined division of labor necessary to produce and direct their own films once they got tired of selling their skills to others.

* * *

One of my favorite stories about Charles Brackett, in a rare example of the fun side of his work with Billy Wilder, is the charming chestnut about the shooting for the film *Ninotchka*. Like nearly every man in America at the time, Brackett had a deep and aching fixation on the sultry and smoldering actress Greta Garbo. Garbo was not amused and Lubitsch became so distracted by the presence of his co-writer gawking, ogling, and otherwise gazing at her during her scenes that he worried it would also distract the icy goddess.

So he and Garbo had a set prop person put up an interior design screen that shielded the star from Brackett's boyish adoration. That seemingly did not dissuade him, however, as he had to endure Billy's terse admonishment upon finding him on all fours and peering up at Greta from below: "Look at you, a grown man clamoring around on the floor gawking at poor Greta like some schoolboy." In all likelihood, however, under the guise of supervising the delivery of their screenplay, Billy too was probably enjoying his coaching of the temperamental star. The fact that Garbo herself was by all accounts a lesbian naturally didn't halt anyone of any gender from falling for her svelte charms.

Brackett was a married family man and a conservative Republican, but his sexuality remains a topic of speculation. William Mann, in his book *Behind the Screen: How Gays and Lesbians Shaped Hollywood*, quotes the British writer and friend of Brackett Gavin

Lambert, who remarks, "I got to know Charlie fairly well. There was a certain subtext between us, we didn't have to discuss it. He knew I was gay, I knew he was." The contention about Brackett is further supported by notable figures such as author Christopher Isherwood and the screenwriter John van Druten, who was a confidant of both Brackett and his daughter's husband Larmore.

That he may have been either gay or bisexual is something we can note briefly but not dwell upon at any length, as it doesn't enter into the core of this narrative. Hollywood was awash with famous players of both genders who had to maintain a sense of prescribed decorum in their public and private lives during the thirties and beyond, often finding themselves on arranged dates or in marriages (such as Rock Hudson's later on) orchestrated by studio matchmakers and publicists intent on maintaining certain illusions of American wholesomeness.

It's an issue that is not really an issue, at least not when considering Brackett's work as a writer, artist, one half of a superior screenwriting team, and, later, a consummately skillful producer. His grandson Jim Moore maintains a respectful distance about this aspect of the man. In his foreword to Brackett's diaries, he writes, "Was he gentle, yes. Could he appear effeminate? Only in that he had a great appreciation for beauty and form, not just in art but in people—men and women. . . . The point is, gay or not, he was a gifted writer, a devoted and self-sacrificing friend, and a loving husband, father, and grandfather."

There is an equivalent reticence demonstrated by the editor of the diaries, Anthony Slide: "What do the diaries and Brackett's published work contain in response to such rumors? In truth, the evidence is as confused as perhaps Brackett himself was in regard to his sexuality." To Slide, much of the commentary regarding Brackett's possible gayness actually "appears to be guilt by association" in the absence of any documentary evidence. But Slide also observes that in Brackett's diaries there are many mentions of gay friends of all sorts, and that his novel *American Colony* was dedicated to a famous gay writer friend, Alexander Woollcott. I agree with Slide that "Ultimately, the issue is not whether Charles Brackett is gay, straight, or bisexual. It is more a matter of whether his sexuality had any relevance to his career as a writer and producer." For me, and for the purposes of this book, it doesn't. End of story.

One thing that is relevant, perhaps the only personal thing, is how he managed to reach a kind of détente, as dizzying as it was, with someone as diametrically opposed to his own temperament as Wilder was, and that's where the wonder of "dinergy"—the union of opposites—comes in. Few people could have been more astonished at the sudden success of *Ninotchka* than Brackett, the apparent fish out of water, since his reserved literary acumen, more suited to the publishing world of New York, was already at odds with the brash and often crass Billy, who was quite at home in the chest-thumping world of celluloid storytelling.

The usually taciturn and even glum Garbo was especially lauded for embodying the shimmering wit of the screenplay for *Ninotchka*, which many considered her quintessential performance, garnering her a third and last Academy Award nomination. The film, naturally, was banned in the Soviet Union and all its satellite states, even later during the war, partially because, ironically, that country was perceived to be helping the Allies fight the Nazis. Frank Nugent, responsible for the great comment "Stalin won't like it," also followed up with "unless your tastes hew too closely to the Party line, we think you will, immensely." Other sly insider jokes include a quip about the fifth five-year plan going well, and Garbo's straight-faced remark, "The last mass trials were a great success. There are going to be fewer but better Russians."

One less satisfying side effect of the film was the impact on Garbo herself, though. Her studio MGM had already scheduled her to play Madame Curie in their upcoming biopic of the scientist, but they were so pleased with the critical and commercial clamor over *Ninotchka*, and especially her repartee with costar Douglas, that they quickly tried to capitalize on it by making another romantic comedy, supposedly in its mold, *Two-Faced Woman*. That film was met with a leaden silence from audiences and critics alike, pelting her with the worst reviews of her long and stellar career. She was so crushed that she retired, feeling that at thirty-five she was now too old to continue acting anyway.

In an ironic sidebar, Brackett and Wilder would try to lure her back into films later on by offering her the role of Norma Desmond in *Sunset Boulevard*, a notion that horrified her, much as it had offended other "elder" actresses they courted, such as Mae West and Pola Negri. A pity, since she would have been remarkable in it, though not nearly as remarkable as the courageous Gloria Swanson. All in all, the notoriety of *Ninotchka* continues to this day, partly because of such delightful Brackett lines as Leon's: "Ninotchka, it's midnight. One half of Paris is making love to the other half." To which Garbo answers, in total deadpan, "Must you flirt?" Leon: "Well I don't have to, but I find it natural." Garbo: "Suppress it."

This global acclaim was not bad at all considering the whole plotline first originated as a three-sentence story idea by Melchior Lengyel, who had been lounging by the swimming pool while MGM executives were looking for a suitable vehicle for Garbo's next picture. He jotted down: "Russian girl saturated with Bolshevist ideals goes to fearful, capitalistic, monopolistic Paris. She meets with romance and has an uproarious good time. Capitalism is not so bad after all." Call it Hollywood's contribution to the Cold War, perhaps. But, naturally, that "not so bad after all" was in reality the recognition of Brackett and Wilder's magic touch—with words, and with each other.

CHAPTER THREE

DREAMTELLERS

Shadowboxing at Night

If I want to send a message, I'll call Western Union.

MITCHELL LEISEN

Naturally, two talented but unseasoned screenwriters could do much worse than to have their first two screen credits being brought to life under the legendary Lubitsch banner, but in the days of the almost industrial dream factory model, writers, along with actors and all other forms of talent, went where they were sent by their bosses. So it was that the studio scribes were called upon to perform emergency surgery on scripts other than their own before returning to form to craft the sparkling gem of *Ninotchka*.

For example, Brackett and Wilder worked on 1938's *That Certain Age*, directed by Edward Ludwig, in between their two notable Lubitsch pictures. A forgettable frolic for which they were loaned out by Paramount to Universal Pictures, it featured Melvyn Douglas and the popular youthful star of many sappy musical comedies and light dramas, Deanna Durbin, with Irene Rich as her mother, John Halliday as her father, and another stalwart youth star of that period, Jackie Cooper. Concocted by screenwriter Bruce Manning from an original story by F. Hugh Herbert, it was something of a paid vacation for Brackett and Wilder, who were "contract writers" and therefore received no credit for their work. Their basic job description more or less consisted of making the script—a light story of teenaged crushes conflated with a "let's put on a musical show" scenario—somewhat less terrible.

By the same business logic, the freshly minted writing team, already beginning to be recognized and acknowledged as something special by an industry that voraciously fed on specialness, would shift their own ambitious attention to another director, Mitchell Leisen. Leisen's *Midnight*, incredibly enough written by the team during the same year they crafted *Ninotchka*, is memorable in a couple of ways, most notably as a showcase for the innate sensibility and skill of the writers at making screwball comedy situations that were quite bonkers but nonetheless came across as strongly human in emotional terms.

Its secondary importance is that it provided a very early experience with the common frustration and disappointment of writers who were under the control of directors capable of altering their screenplays at whim. The animosity seeded during this exposure to the rampant egos and unequal politics of the Hollywood hierarchy would instill in Brackett and Wilder a burning desire to assume control of their own creative material. They would achieve this creative freedom eventually, by personally and professionally assuming the dual roles of writer-producer and writer-director, but first they needed to pay their dues in the trenches. And in many ways, their labors indicated that they may even have overpaid.

Midnight was another classic screwball romp, frantic and antic, yet still somehow believable in a surreal sort of way, mostly due to the deft characterizations and comedic skills of Don Ameche and Claudette Colbert (who took over the role from a designated Barbara Stanwyck due to scheduling difficulties). Colbert is an unemployed and stranded American showgirl in Paris who is hired by a wealthy patron to break up his wife's adulterous affair. She is basically homeless and penniless but charming enough to convince a kindly Hungarian taxi driver named Tibor, played perfectly by the effortlessly brilliant Ameche, to chauffeur her around to nightclubs in search of a job.

Ameche's taxi driver is kind enough, and apparently trusting enough, to offer his apartment for her to stay over while he roams the city during his night shift. She thinks better of the idea and slips off into the rainy Parisian night, only to find herself seeking shelter at a black-tie classical concert. A series of speedy misunderstandings results in her about to be discovered and unmasked as an imposter when John Barrymore (playing his usual Barrymore persona) helps her by stuffing a wad of cash into her purse and then escorts her to a lavish hotel suite he has booked for her. Needless to say, his intentions are nowhere near as honorable as those of Tibor, who, now smitten with Colbert's charms, launches himself into a frenzied search across the city of lights, enlisting the aid of an army of his fellow cabdrivers by inventing a betting pool and charging his pals a nominal fee to go out and find the missing lady and win the pot full of cash.

Eventually, she is found safe and sound, of course, while in the process of agreeing to marry one or more several well-heeled men to ameliorate her tenuous financial status, but inevitably Ameche professes his ardent love for her, she responds in kind, and the two head off to a marriage bureau, leaving his army of cabbie friends satisfied with a good deed done, and with one of them raking in his pool winnings. The film was remade six years later as in *Masquerade in Mexico* with Dorothy Lamour, and as of 2011 was slated for a potential remake again as a vehicle for Reese Witherspoon, but that pipe dream has yet to materialize. Reese, of course, is certainly no Claudette.

There's a reason this film was later selected by the Library of Congress's National Film Registry as being "culturally, historically, and aesthetically significant." When *Midnight* opened on March 1939, it was greeted with a veritable flood of adulation and admiring reviews, with one particular piece in *Motion Picture Daily* drawing attention to the fact that though Brackett, Wilder, and Leisen had fought like cats and dogs during production, and that even the characters onscreen frequently resorted to physical persuasion, the official screening of the film was a notable "love fest" of mutual cooing: "This is, in fact, just about the best light comedy ever caught by a camera . . . when a cross-industry turnout enjoyed its preview screening with that wholesome, whole-hearted enthusiasm which, about once a year, erases company boundaries, banishes professional prejudices, and makes of a top-flight Hollywood audience a mere theatreful of completely contented film fans for a night. It takes a pretty fine piece of entertainment to do that." From film historian Ed Sikov's perspective, summing it up in his book *Life and Times of Wilder*, Brackett and Wilder "became the hottest screenwriting team in town."

They were now, in an aptly ironic Sikov characterization, "coupled." If that intriguing term connotes a kind of subtle bondage, I suspect that was the intention. But if the feverishly lauded team's almost sadomasochistic character became legendary, their dynamic was always suspended in tandem and an even more exotic form of threesome: the love-hate relationship they would share with their producer-directors in those early days. At this stage, Mitchell Leisen (1898–1972) was renowned as a highly capable director from the same Golden Age school of filmmaking as Ernst Lubitsch, but the American campus. Hailing from Michigan, he entered the film industry while it was practically still in its infancy in the 1920s, originally toiling as a costume designer, then art director, and finally as a director. Specializing in glossy melodramas and screwball farces which often lampooned the romantic comedy styles of which they were a subgenre, his first film was the 1933 pre-code drama *Cradle Song*.

Even after the new Hollywood moral code came into effect, he proved himself adept at subverting it. His best-known films were *Death Takes a Holiday* and *Murder at the Vanities* (both 1934) and the Preston Sturges films *Easy Living* (1937) and *Remember the Night* (1940), the last film written by Sturges before he moved into directing his own works. Leisen would later direct three of Brackett and Wilder's scripts (and one of Brackett's solo comedies, *The Mating Season*, in 1951 after they split up). Equally adept at both screwball comedy and melodramas which were accidental comedies, a great deal of his reputation was the result of the by then accomplished Brackett and Wilder franchise. They would also contribute greatly to a later wartime drama that brought about a rupture with the director over his persistent tampering with their screenplays.

Over time, many of Leisen's apparently lighthearted movies have been getting more serious critical attention by writers able to glimpse beneath the bright and shiny surface he specialized in mining. Dave Kehr, writing in the *New York Times* in 2008 about *The Big Trail*, and reviewing *Midnight*, characterized him as the "very model of the crack studio director . . . [spending] most of his career at Paramount, where he tackled projects as radically different as the archly theatrical *Death Takes a Holiday* (1934) and the frothy revue film *The Big Broadcast of 1938* with the same composure and elegance." In addition, David Melville, for instance, in the film journal *Senses of Cinema*, has contributed to this ongoing reassessment: "Leisen, glimpsed in a new light, is no longer a swishy hack. He's a subtle and stylish auteur who could add heart and humanity to the brittle sophistication of Billy Wilder."

Mark Rappaport, writing an essay in *Rouge* for a Cinematheque Française retrospective of Leisen's works, had some tantalizing speculations about how some of Billy Wilder and Charles Brackett's scripts would have come across if Wilder had already taken to directing himself. The answer he proposed was: not nearly as well.

Yet, that was exactly the power struggle that eventually sank the Leisen/Brackett/Wilder enterprise, although it took three films to capsize entirely.

*   *   *

If Leisen could be considered the "model of a crack studio director" during these early years of their collaborations together, Brackett and Wilder became justly renowned as crack studio writers, even if they didn't always applaud the projects they were forced to undertake as salary slaves. In the year 1939, the beginning of their golden age together, they still had to survive working on other people's screenplays, repairing and spicing up scripts which were far inferior to their own original work. Thus, their uncredited toil on *What a Life* (1939), directed by Theodore Reed, in between their second and third outings under Leisen, followed up by drudge work developing story treatments such as that for *French Without Tears* (1940), directed by Anthony Asquith, and rendering them largely anonymous. That same year though, even while enduring the physically draining and soul-crushing merry-go-round of the studio contract writer's life, they still managed to pull off another sparkling screenplay for yet more Leisen antics.

The title of Leisen's 1940 film *Arise My Love* comes from the Song of Solomon: "Arise my love, my fair one, and come away with me." The shooting began on June 24, 1940 and continued until mid-August, while the screenplay, with an interventionist ethos fairly unusual for the time, underwent constant alterations to enable the inclusion of actual current events of note, such as the sinking of the SS *Athenia* and the armistice between France and Germany in the Forest of Compiegne.

Private events and personal experiences leading up to the writing and filming of their second Leisen feature were deeply traumatic for the Wilder family. They had been living in a rented apartment in

Beverly Hills, but in November 1939 had purchased a charming little property and planned to build a house in Bel Air. Just before Christmas, Wilder's wife Judith gave birth to twins, Vincent and Victoria. He immediately went back to work on a project involving more literary renovation than actual writing, a Bing Crosby musical called (at the time) *Ghost Music*, which went through so many convolutions and permutations—including Bing's own writing team being parachuted in—that it was hardly recognizable when it was released as *Rhythm of the River*. Wilder's contributions had mostly evaporated, which he didn't mind much at all.

In early March, shortly after Brackett, Wilder, and Reisch were honored with their first Oscar nomination for *Ninotchka*, the Wilder's family physician declared that the twins were thriving. But then, suddenly on the last day of March, Vincent passed away from a condition that had prevented his lungs from growing properly. Three-month-old Vincent Wilder was cremated on April 2, and perhaps as a means of surviving the traumatic loss, Wilder was already back at work by June. As Ed Sikov observes, Wilder coped in a classic manner by submerging or sublimating his grief and his knowledge of the calamitous upheaval back in his homeland: "Added to the typical turmoil of Billy's partnership with Brackett, these new tensions meant that life at the office was even more dangerous than usual. There was, needless to say, lots of yelling."

The storyline of *Arise*, with its parallel tracks of basic romance and incendiary wartime tale, was not exactly to everyone's liking, with critic Bosley Crowther of the *New York Times* complaining that it was basically a synthetic rendering of a simple April-in-Paris theme, one that attempted narrative consequence by inserting the realities of war: "Miss Colbert and Mr. Milland are very charming when tete-a-tete, but with Europe going up in flames around them, they are, paradoxically, not so hot." But his reading of the story and its presentation may clearly have been colored somewhat, quite fairly perhaps, by the alarm with which European events were being viewed from the distance of America.

In retrospect, however, its value, like many romantic comedies set in a dramatic terrain, has evolved over time. The Colbert character of Augusta Nash was reportedly based upon real life war journalist and Hemingway lover Martha Gellhorn, and it reminds us today of the salient fact that even in times of utter madness, and against all odds for a humanity under violent threat by tyranny, something as simple as love just still happens to happen. The only slightly over-the-top narrative won a Best Story Oscar for Benjamin Glazer and Hans Szekely, with nominations for Victor Young's intense music, Charles Lang's cinematography, and Hans Dreir and Robert Usher's art direction.

Wilder was perpetually irritated by Leisen from the very beginning of their liaison: "Brackett and I sweated for a long time on our scripts so they would work. Then Leisen would drop a line or a whole page, or he would let some actress say whatever she wanted. Here we were setting up for the big payoff in our story, and he was sabotaging us. . . . I challenged Leisen and producer Arthur Hornblow demanded that I be banned from the set. That made me more determined." When the film was released in fall of 1940 to much acclaim, the fallout with Leisen continued, with the director telling the press that the film was "Charlie Brackett at his best," completely disregarding the fact that Wilder was the movie's coauthor.

As melodramatic as Leisen's saga was (he was often compared to Douglas Sirk in that regard) it was actually based on the true story of one Harold Dahl, a pilot who was shot down while flying in the Spanish Civil War for the Republican Air Force and initially was sentenced to be executed. Diplomatic gestures included a personal visit to Francisco Franco on the part of Dahl's impressively beautiful singer-wife, Edith Rogers. He remained in prison until he was released in 1940 and allowed to return to America. The love story between the pilot and a journalist was known to be among Claudette Colbert's favorites. In the film version, the pilot joins the RAF to fight in France, while Colbert's journalist remains there as a war correspondent. Subsequent to the fall of Paris, both choose to return home to America, expressly to convince its citizens and government that a serious global cataclysm of epic proportions is on the way. And indeed it was.

In addition to several excellent books on Leisen—chief among them a 1973 biography by David Chierichetti called *Leisen: Hollywood Director*—his contemporary rehabilitation as a serious cinematic artist has been further explored by David Melville for *Senses of Cinema*, in which he lamented the fact that when Leisen passed away in 1972 at the Motion Picture Country Home, his films and his life had been mostly bypassed and forgotten: "One of a host of old-style Hollywood directors who had not been rediscovered, re-interpreted, or (in some cases) re-created as an auteur by *Cahiers du Cinéma*, Leisen was remembered, grudgingly, as a minor artisan."

He was, however, a subtle artist whose actual strenuous efforts were so invisible that he was deemed too effortless to be taken seriously. This mistake was made most egregiously by film historian Steven Bach, who austerely claimed that "Leisen was competent and stylish at his best. He could always make a picture *look* better than it was, but never *play* better." For Melville, by contrast, Leisen's "wild dream sequences are as close to the avant-garde as 1940s Hollywood could allow." He goes even further, and in a way with which I concur, making a case that Leisen might in fact be the first postmodern filmmaker, as nearly none of his movies can be interpreted as being within a single genre or frame of reference. In that regard he is similar in many respects to another fervid master of all trades in Hollywood, the brilliant Michael Curtiz, about whom I have written elsewhere.

The dismissals of Leisen's work at the time were condescending, if benign, compared to the assessments of the two screenwriters, whose early careers were largely constructed on the scripts they wrote for him, the ones with which he tinkered and so easily enraged Wilder and Brackett. Billy Wilder once claimed he would never watch a film by a director on the lesser medium of television, unless it was a picture by a someone he hated, adding that there was *no* director he hated *that* much, not even Mitchell Leisen.

Yet Leisen, the director with whom they both had moments of pique, seemed to have his finger on the pulse of their convoluted magic, as he indicated in his own memoir, *Hollywood Director*: "Writing a script with Charles Brackett and Billy was very hard work, but we got results. We had daily meetings and built the thing up slowly, sequence by sequence, arguing all the way. . . . Brackett was sort of a leveling influence. He would referee my quarrels with Billy. As a team, they were the greatest."

Wilder, naturally, disagreed with Leisen's own interpretation of their day-to-day reality: "Charlie never was a peacemaker. That's bullshit. It was Arthur Hornblow [their producer at that stage] who refereed our fights. Charlie hated him as much as I did. All he did was he fucked up the script, and our scripts were damn near perfection." Needless to say, Leisen had just as much disdain for Wilder, an artist he found impossible to either manage or dominate to his own directorial satisfaction. Sooner or later, everyone who ever worked with Billy reached the same conclusion, even if they adored him: he would not be supervised to any degree when it came to making his words come to life on the screen.

*   *   *

Michael Felsher's astute description of another combustible cinematic couple, the German director Werner Herzog and his incendiary actor alter-ago Klaus Kinski, as "two highly charged particles of celluloid energy" is equally apt in the case of the Brackett and Wilder roller coaster ride through a captivating carnival of laughter and tears. From the moment these two particular particles were thrown together by Paramount Studios under the tutelage of Lubitsch, two things quickly became apparent, to them at least. First: some sort of unique electromagnetic spark happened when they wrote together, and it could happen regardless of which director they worked for; second: their ambition was such that they both believed they could be a success in Hollywood, especially if they took control of their own material.

But though they both thought they could make a go of it in the convoluted jungle of Hollywood egos, it may never have fully occurred to them that their success would in part rest on having the stamina to stay together and let their creative spark run its course. Such was their unconscious insight, seemingly beyond, below, or above the personal level of shared animosity, that they succeed in recognizing their own brand together and even elevate it to a corporate status worthy of maintenance, no matter what the personal cost. They rapidly realized that working together, as distressing as it might be, was the only means to reaching that obscure magic that is so often only available by *looking through* one's partner's eyes.

Once two people establish a bond that unites them creatively, and especially if they achieve a huge degree of success, wealth, and recognition, breaking up is not only hard to do, it's often impossible. In short, it suggests that a psychological compromise is equally essential for both parties, one that enables the team itself to thrive rather than one member or the other. The motivation for creative collaborators to engage in such a compromise? Surprisingly, that motivation is provided by all of us, their audience. We want them to resolve their differences because we want watch their films, and we reward them accordingly if they do so. Even if it's only for thirteen difficult years and thirteen great movies.

A huge number of Brackett diary entries throughout 1940 are either illegible and impossible to transcribe, possibly having been scribbled under extreme duress, or else are riddled with repeated uses of the word "sterile" to describe their studio office working days. They range from ennui in August—"Unprofitable day at the studio discussing possibilities."—to angst in October: "At the office Billy was very averse to work, finally saying it was punishment of God on a Jew for trying to work on Yom Kippur." I can't help thinking that apart from whatever traumas were lodged in Wilder's brain, he also seemed to be suffering from some sort of drastic inferiority complex, one that manifested itself in obscure insecurities about his work, perhaps causing an overcompensation through inflated egomania.

And this despite the fact that even though he was not yet fluent in English (his speech remained idiosyncratic throughout his life), he still possessed a fiery brilliance for story invention and character interplay. Or perhaps it's more accurate to say that he was possessed by it. Brackett's entries in spring 1941 repeatedly describe Wilder as unable to work. On March 30, Wilder's wife "called to say that Billy 'was having a nervous breakdown,' to my horror and relief."

The overlapping operatic behavior, existential edginess, and perpetual planning for the next picture—while two others were still either being developed, finished, or dormant—must have been excruciating for both partners, though they managed to display the stress in quite different ways. They carried this baggage with them into their conference meetings with director Howard Hawks, who had agreed to undertake *Ball of Fire*, although he expressed reservations about the fact that their heroine, Barbara Stanwyck, had been cast as the mistress of a villainous gangster (which was, of course, the crux of the whole story). Hawks came to one grim conference with the writers to discuss potentially casting Lucille Ball, who Hawks considered unworthy of the role. Brackett recalled Hawks saying that the "trouble is the script is too funny." Whereas

Brackett hoped Ball, or even Ginger Rogers, would be given the role of Sugarpuss, which eventually went to Stanwyck, whom he considered "a pleasant, heavy-faced girl, very wrong." I couldn't disagree more: Stanwyck could act circles around Ball and Rogers, and did finally, in the end.

Considering how racy, saucy, chipper, and up-tempo *Ball of Fire* turned out in the end, it is surprising to find out how laborious, anxiety-drenched, and fraught the whole experience of creating that magical scenario could be. On July 3, Brackett wrote, "Today it was Billy's neurosis which kept us from rewriting our sequence. He wanted it virtually new, with a new emphasis that he couldn't find. As a result, nothing was written and our nerves were in fringes. A day at Howard Hawks' is always a day of hell."

Wilder seemed to already have a great deal in common with Hawks, though, particularly taste-wise and in what he wanted to see on the screen. As Wilder recalled, "He was a good director. His touch was light and the audience was not aware of the picture being directed by anyone. Everything seemed natural and easy, but it wasn't natural and easy for him. Hawks was a fumbler, a hair-splitter, but that wasn't the character he played on the set." Early on, Wilder learned the technique of "cutting in the camera," a concise method he definitely picked up by the shoulder of Hawks: "It's the scissors that make the picture. Cutting is very, very important. It's the juxtaposition of the various shots that makes the picture, so what I do is try not to give them any extra film to monkey around with."

By November, and true to form, even before *Ball of Fire* had premiered, the writing partners would be engaged with the fresh hell of manifesting Wilder's first directorial outing, *The Major and the Minor*. Brackett found some solace in eventually working with Ginger Rogers, even if it meant also working with Wilder, who now would have the double boost to his ego of being both co-writer *and* director. Billy was still however, careful and cautious about his directorial debut, recalling that "everybody was sure I was going to do some German Expressionist thing sure to fail, and that crazy Wilder would go back to his typewriter and stop bothering everybody. But I was very careful. I set out to make a commercial picture I wouldn't be ashamed of, so my first picture as a director wouldn't be my last."

By December 10, according to Brackett, the overall working tone was set: "A loathsome day . . . I said to Billy, 'Don't you think we ought to do a little work?' Whereupon there was a scene. The morning was lost." The following day, Germany declared war on the United States. "Billy and I were very gay, but unproductive." In other words, everything was proceeding according to plan: ominous, gay, unproductive.

But writers for hire quickly tire, especially of each other. The celluloid straw that finally broke the writers' backs was a twofold blessing in disguise. Earlier they had passed up the opportunity to write a Bob Hope comedy vehicle, possibly because of the darkness in Wilder's private life and the team's general demeanor regarding the apparent impending collapse of Western civilization, and chose instead to endure yet another Leisen venture. A glum but strangely, and ironically, witty black comedy about a stranded refugee caught in a no-man's-land between two equally unwelcoming countries, 1941's *Hold Back the Dawn* was based on a Ketti Frings story crafted that same year. I might be the only one who classifies it as a black comedy, but then, I'm also one of the few who finds the real appeal of *Sunset Boulevard* to be in its barely concealed satire and parody of moviemaking in general and Hollywood in particular. (Besides, Wilder and Brackett have both gone on record as stating that that later film was also originally a comedy, of sorts, though in my opinion it also never stopped being one, despite its obvious tragic contours.)

Brackett and Wilder were again dismayed by the changes made to their script. Pushed over the edge by both studio and directorial interference, Wilder in particular was furious. After Leisen followed his usual pattern of needing to control every aspect of a film he was crafting, including and perhaps especially the stellar scripts he came to take for granted from the studio contract writers at his disposal, Wilder pledged that he would soon take the reins and direct the films whose stories they wrote and he also encouraged the reluctant Brackett to eventually take the wheel as producer. Brackett was astute enough to know that this would merely place him in the same hazardous position as he had been with both Lubitsch and Leisen, but with the even scarier prospect of a dominant Billy Wilder commanding the set with whip in hand: "I find myself fretting at the prospect of becoming Billy's stooge producer—a prospect I detest."

But before they could entertain Wilder's plan, they had to survive their current movie together. There were the usual on-set troubles with certain stubborn actors who unfortunately were stars, and behind the scenes with a director who unfortunately was Mitchell Leisen. Along with the storyline details, the character played by Charles Boyer in particular went through a series of evolutions until he devolved into the darkly arch scoundrel Georges Iscovescu, a Romanian gigolo. As the film opens, in a curious reverse echo of their future satire on Hollywood itself, the Boyer character arrives at the Paramount Pictures studio lot, trying anxiously to meet a film director named Saxon (who was played by Leisen himself). Iscovescu claims to have a true story to tell, his own, for $500. The rest of the film emerges slowly and in still comically sinister tones, in flashback sequences unfolding within the Boyer character's pitched story.

The gigolo role seemed tailor-made for the smooth but slightly unctuous Boyer, who marries an American woman while stranded in Mexico in order to have access to America but ends up actually falling in love with her. Along with other hopeful refugees, he must wait for an inordinately long time to get a quota number, and he dwells in a kind of obscure limbo in the Esperanza Hotel. Six months interred there finds him depressed and totally broke, with nothing but his romantic skills to fall back on. These talents he calls upon after meeting an ex-lover who explains that she gained US citizenship by marrying an American and then rapidly divorcing him.

Olivia de Havilland is perfectly cast as the earnest and innocent schoolteacher he chooses as his victim. Boyer's character is thwarted by the same former lover, and expert gold digger, who had alerted him to the nefarious idea in the first place. She still loves him and cruelly divulges the whole plan to de Havilland's Emmy, who becomes ill with the news and has a car accident back in the United States. Georges is so overcome with what appears to be regret that he illegally enters America to visit and nurse her back to health. With immigration authorities now on his trail he returns mournfully to Mexico, where he fully expects to live in oblivion forever, but first he stops at the Paramount studio office to try to entice Leisen's director to buy his story.

But this is Hollywood, after all, not Mexico. Back on the beach at the border town, Georges learns that his illegal entry had not been reported and that his visa is now granted. In a final scene of sheer but blissful schmaltz worthy of Leisen at his Sirk-like melodramatic best, Georges looks from the sand he had been staring at, only to see Emmy bathed in blazing sunlight in a summer hat, waving ecstatically to him from across the border, which he crosses to reunite with her. They walk off together, in search of a shared America, having established a bond that, shockingly enough to the former gigolo, is no longer a pretense. *Variety* observed that "While *Hold Back the Dawn* is basically another European refugee yarn, scenarists Charles Brackett and Billy Wilder exercised some ingenuity and imagination and Ketti Frings' original emerges as fine celluloidia."

Over the course of the making of *Hold Back the Dawn*, Brackett and Wilder developed a loathing not just for Leisen but for Boyer. As Wilder recalled about a scene in which Georges sits in a prison cell,

"Brackett and I are having lunch at the restaurant across the street from Paramount, and there is Boyer having lunch. And I say, what are you shooting today? He says, 'We are shooting the scene with the cockroach, but we changed it a little, I do not talk to the cockroach anymore because that is stupid. How can I talk to a cockroach when a cockroach cannot answer me.' I was really furious and on the way out I said to Brackett, 'That son of a bitch, if he don't talk to a cockroach, he don't talk to nobody!' We went back and finished the third act, and we gave everything to Olivia de Havilland."

This is one of those rare but delicious examples of the occasional power a screenwriter might wield against an egotistical actor—one too thick to realize that his suave and charming character, having been abandoned by the world while he rotted in lonely confinement, would naturally be reduced to chatting to his only friend, an insect. That one scene alone would have humanized the otherwise dour and conniving con man and created a sympathy for his plight with the audience that he would otherwise not have had. Revenge can sometimes be sweet for those nervous artisans who create our alternate realities.

CHAPTER FOUR

INDEPENDENCE DAY

You Don't Own Me

Don't blame me, I'm not an executive, I'm only a writer.
WILLIAM HOLDEN AS JOE GILLIS IN *SUNSET BOULEVARD*

Although comedy in various forms has existed, if not since time immemorial then at least since Aristophanes started snoring during a Socrates dissertation, it was in the twentieth century that it rose to an imperial kind of prominence formerly only accorded to drama and tragedy. This may, of course, have been due to the fact that that century was one of the saddest and most woe-begotten periods in human history since the medieval era, or it may also have been since the industrial age saw the transmission of images and stories provoking laughter reach a peak level of mass distribution. And Hollywood was naturally the epicenter of that huge pop culture wave, just as its designers intended that it should be. So, the invention of the comedic art was one thing, but the perfecting of its codes was yet another.

One of the finest explorations of the unique parameters of modern and contemporary comedy was penned by Steve Vineberg, in his *High Comedy in American Movies: Class and Humor from the 1920s to the Present*: "High comedy, also known as comedy of manners, was invented by the British Restoration playwrights in the late seventeenth century. Conventionally, high comedy is elevated in both style and subject matter, and class is a felicitously inescapable boundary. When most people hear the term 'high comedy' they think of *The Importance of Being Earnest*, or the plays of Noël Coward. But we Americans have our own high comic playwrights, whose period of popularity came between the two world wars. And what makes American comedy of manners so fascinating is the ways in which American identity—historically in tension with the distinctly undemocratic substance of the high-comic universe—interacts with that universe to produce a series of variations on the genre."

In Vineberg's fine study, the reader is taken on a guided tour of the comedic traditions as uniquely exemplified by the Yankee sensibility: "High comedy is one of several comic genres known to American audiences; the others are romantic comedy, burlesque, hardboiled comedy, sentimental comedy, parody, black comedy, satire, and farce." Clearly what Robert Corrigan, in his comedy, *Meaning and Form*, characterized as the comic spirit, and its national muse, is almost as varied as the complexities of American character itself. Another useful insight into tensions between high and low forms was provided by playwright S. N. Berman in a 1952 *New York Times* article, "Query: What Makes Comedy High?": "The immediate concern of the characters in a high comedy may sometimes be trivial; high comedy is seriousness of temperament and intensity of purpose in contrast with the triviality of the occasion."

Vineberg also further reminded us that "High comedy is a very delicately crafted thing—a soufflé. In order to work best it must be as light as gossamer and seem easy and slight and entirely superficial; that's how writers and directors produced what, in Pauline Kael's view, Lubitch produced: 'almost perfectly preserved iridescent make-believe worlds'. What the finest high comedies accomplish is to seem superficial while actually being profound." Indeed, that is precisely the most ideal gauge by which to calibrate the curious paradox in Brackett-Wilder screenplays for directors as diverse as Lubitsch, Leisen, and Hawks, or even their own original works such as *The Major and the Minor*, as well as several films they wrote and produced independent of each other after their creative divorce.

As difficult as it is to believe in today's jaded and fiscally out-of-whack film industry, where artists work obsessively and laboriously for several years on a new project, 1941 saw the screenwriting team working on two great films for two great but drastically different directors, simultaneously. *Hold Back the Dawn* came out at the end of September, while their first film written for the notoriously tough taskmaster Howard Hawks premiered at the beginning of December. It would have been an incredible feat of both stamina and talent on the part of even the most blessed writers, but for his part, Wilder was already determined to find a way out of the cul-de-sac of near-medieval toil that studio writing embodied during the Golden Age he helped inaugurate. And as rough and tumble as Hawks was known to be, a voluble director in the tough-guy, hard-drinking John Ford mode of operation, he still recognized grit and gifted ambition when he saw it.

Hawks was also smart enough to realize that he would benefit from even better screenplays if he also let the hungry Wilder apprentice with him on the set and study close up what it meant to be a director, even if it meant he would be literally manufacturing his next industry competitor at the same time. So, just as he had more or less learned the English language from his writing partner Brackett, Wilder studied the language of directorial aesthetics from Hawks. It would be a banner year for both partners. After working with Lubitsch and Leisen, the writing team was more than ready to deliver a genuinely masterful screenplay to a director who was an acknowledged master and a maker of genuine masterpieces. He was also a director who truly appreciated great writers.

Howard Hawks (1896–1977), the man who critic Leonard Maltin once called "the greatest American director who is not a household name," was a towering figure in the Golden Age of Hollywood, someone who had done just about every job involved in making movies with the exception of being a movie star. Perhaps the most stylistically versatile director ever, he preferred making other people stars, and also bringing exceptional screenplays to life on the screen with an accomplished sense of artful ease. Having made excellent works in every genre—everything from comedies, dramas, and science fiction to film noir, war films, and westerns—with equal aplomb, he was also notable for his cinematic portrayals of powerful and tough-talking female characters, the kind who became known as "Hawksian women," even though he himself was not one to espouse feminism per se. His films have influenced a group of contemporary auteurs as disparate as Martin Scorsese, Robert Altman, Jean-Luc Godard, and John Carpenter, to name but a few.

While working at odd jobs in the film industry as a wide-eyed twenty-year-old in 1916 during his summer vacation, Hawks had fallen in love with the prospect of involving himself with movies in any way, shape, or form. Slightly delayed by his enrollment in the Aviation Section of the US Army Signal Corps but before he could be called up for active duty, he returned to Hollywood and by the end of 1917 was, incredibly enough, working on a Cecil B. DeMille film before even finishing college.

Hawks's ingenuity, resourcefulness, and self-confidence were established early on in his amazingly long and fruitful career. After meeting cinematographer Victor Fleming in 1916 he scored his first job as a prop boy on a Douglas Fairbanks film. According to Fleming, when a new set was required quickly and the designer was unavailable, Hawks volunteered to take on the task himself. Following this he became a general assistant to DeMille and eventually was working on one of the great man's films and also contributing to a

Mary Pickford movie. As Hawks tells it, the director of the Pickford film didn't show up for work one day and, ever-resourceful, he volunteered to take on the task of directing a scene or two. Eventually he directed his first film sequence at the age of twenty-one, again with Pickford. Not a bad beginning to a legendary career.

After World War I, Hawks took up residence in Hollywood and never looked back. He apparently utilized some of his family's wealth to loan money to studio mogul Sam Goldwyn, a good man to have in your debt. Goldwyn paid off the debt and added a unique form of interest, hiring him to produce a series of one-reel comedies, following which Hawks formed his own production company and was more or less off to the races. Famous Players Film Company president Jesse Lasky was looking for a new production editor in the story department, and Irving Thalberg recommended Hawks. In 1925, Hawks joined Fox Films and commenced his directing run of eight films in three years.

By 1930, Hollywood was in an uproar over the arrival of talking pictures, a development which Hawks merely took in stride, directing his first sound film, *Dawn Patrol*, with Douglas Fairbanks Jr. That year also saw fabled mogul Howard Hughes hire Hawks to produce the pre-code masterpiece *Scarface*, with Paul Muni. Fond of moving from one studio to another as it suited his vast ambitions, Hawks shifted to Columbia Pictures and made his first screwball comedy, *Twentieth Century*, with John Barrymore and Carole Lombard, which is considered the defining film of the screwball genre. After a string of rapid-fire productions, he directed another classic screwball achievement, *Bringing Up Baby*, for RKO Pictures. He followed up with a string of eleven straight consecutive hits which few could match for their mastery of multiple styles, stories, and aesthetic qualities.

Returning the favor to Jesse Lasky for his early support, in 1941 Hawks agreed to cast Gary Cooper as the pacifist farmer who becomes a decorated sharpshooting soldier in *Sergeant York*, the highest-grossing film of that year and one that garnered two Academy Awards, for Best Actor and Best Film Editing, as well as earning Hawks his single nomination as Best Director. Later the same year, Hawks would work with Cooper again in a totally different genre once again, the topsy-turvy brilliance of *Ball of Fire*.

Howard Hawks was not only a force of nature, he was a genius, one who I personally believe to be the greatest American filmmaker ever (yes, and for me, even more so that Orson Welles) due to the sheer diversity and virtuosity of his artistic vision—not to mention his skill in creating commercial blockbusters while still honing the craft of cinematic storytelling. Throughout he maintained a reverence for the story itself and a respect for screenwriters (having practiced even that craft as well during his emergence). Hawks was, in a manner similar to Hitchcock, the kind of artful director who directed his films completely in his mind, and on paper, as he went through the motions of bringing them to life. Many historians have observed that, unlike other directors, even many highly competent ones, the films of Hawks were not collaged together in the cutting room, but rather took shape literally in his feverish brain, to such a high degree that no editor would ever be able to alter them much later on.

He also had an appreciation for the importance of mentoring up-and-coming practitioners the way he himself had been helped. He was therefore not only amenable and open to letting the still-evolving Billy Wilder shadow him on set and take notes about the directorial arts and sciences; he encouraged the eager writer to do so, possibly seeing in him an echo of his own ambitious rise.

Ball of Fire is not only one of my favorite Brackett/Wilder films, second only perhaps to *The Lost Weekend* and *Sunset Boulevard* (which are technically really more *their* films), but might even be one of my favorite films by anyone anywhere. It is almost perfect in

every way, mostly owing, of course, to the masterful way that Howard Hawks embodied their screenplay. I suppose I first fell in love
with it because I also fell in love with its costar Barbara Stanwyck
while watching in the middle of the night as an eleven-year-old boy
(the perfect age to encounter Stanwyck's saucy and spunky dame
archetype). My love affair with her was stubborn, even lasting all the
way into her silver-haired portrayal of the ranch matriarch Victoria
Barclay in *The Big Valley*.

In the ideally titled *Ball of Fire*, Stanwyck would be on the receiving end of some cheeky dialogue delivered by Cooper's Professor
Potts, lines that completely summed up my prepubescent admira-
tion for the paradoxical charms of her Sugarpuss character. ("Make
no mistake. I shall regret the absence of your keen mind. Unfortunately, it is inseparable from an extremely disturbing body." That
was in all likelihood a Brackett-concocted confection.) At any rate,
the film is perfect from start to finish, and along with *Ninotchka*, is
also a consummate screwball work of art. It is also one which has
the double-edged advantage of being the film where Billy Wilder
was tutored on how to direct a movie by a genius professor himself,
Howard Hawks.

*   *   *

Another valuable expedition into this nebulous creative territory
was conducted by the editors of *Classical Hollywood Comedy*, Kristine Karnick and Henry Jenkins, in which they examined a diverse
range of issues relating to genre and narrative in Hollywood comedies, including melodrama, spectacle, and the redefinition of gender
in screwball comedy. As they astutely point out in their introduction, "Nostalgia is a powerful emotional force, a central element
in our experience of films. . . . Nostalgia works by simplifying the
past, removing all contradictions and nuances in favor of an oft-
told narrative of innocence lost. The 'infantile' quality of comedy, its

presocial or antisocial impulses harkening back to the unregulated urges of childhood, makes it a ripe field for nostalgic recollection."

That "immediate experience" of popular culture is precisely the one we need to embrace to fully appreciate the anarchic elements inherent to great comedy, with both *Midnight* and *The Major and the Minor* being prime examples. The latter film, the first written/ produced/directed by the Brackett-Wilder collaborative equation, managed to simultaneously celebrate both the innocence of comedy and the nostalgia for childhood at the same time, all brilliantly wrapped up in the surreal conventions of the screwball genre. Genre films are, by the way, not a lesser domain somehow distinct from the "masterpiece" traditions, as Mary Beth Haralovich clarifies so well: "Genre films sell themselves to audiences not on the basis of their meaning as particular films but because they meet audience expectations generated by their genre conventions."

Karnick and Jenkins further elaborate however, that "comedy's dependence upon stereotypical characters and situations would be one example of the way that redundancy gets built into the systems of genres. Yet at the same time, the absence of novelty would make the repeated consumption of genre films a pleasureless activity. If genres provide the framework of shared assumptions which make a popular film understandable, genre also defines the space for potential innovation and invention." The same authors also emphasize that despite their adherence to, if not conformity with, classical norms, romance-based satires and parodies still offer us an ample space for excess, virtuosity, and spectacle. As James Naremore has suggested, "Classical films often provided plot rationales for the layering of identities, for impersonation or masquerade, which allow their stars to display their performance skills."

I would also note in addition that films that highlight impersonation and masquerade, such as *Ninotchka*, *Midnight*, *Ball of Fire*, and *The Major and the Minor* are almost supreme examples of a theatrical convention being adhered to and subverted at the same time. In discussing Frank Capra's *It Happened One Night*, Jenkins observes accurately that the built-in absurdity of impersonation mimics acting itself, to begin with, but also presents a perfect opportunity to showcase linguistic highwire skills: "The bantering dialogue and rapid delivery which characterizes screwball comedy has been linked to the film's overall conception of male-female relationships . . . The smooth interaction between two performers can suggest how much these characters belong together."

Of particular interest to our exploration, Jenkins also stresses that contrasting performance styles, such as what he calls the "sizzling 'hot' sexuality of Barbara Stanwyck . . . and the more pedestrian qualities of her costars (Gary Cooper, Henry Fonda) . . . indicate issues which must be resolved before the couple can be brought together. The sound of the actor's voices (Cooper's tongue-tiedness, the clicking of Stanwyck's tongue and suggestiveness of her slangy talk); their physical appearance (the glistening of her hair, the shimmer of her legs); and the movements of their bodies (her hip-swinging walk, his nervous stumble) all help to define the interplay between these two characters." Such a nimble insight in body language further reveals what the critic Pauline Kael described as "That sustained feat of careless magic we call thirties comedy."

Even more importantly, and as stressed by Tina Lent, "Screwball comedy redefined film comedy of the 1930s and the conventions of this new genre were the third major source for the modification of the portrayal of gender relations on the Hollywood screen. . . . The romantic leads often had eccentric qualities, and their unconventional behavior was both a form of social criticism and anarchic individualism." Oddly enough, however, social criticism and anarchic individualism would be echoed a little later on in film noir depictions of tragedy, further spotlighting the peculiar bond between laughter and tears. But, as James Harvey astutely declared in his wonderful study *Romantic Comedy in Hollywood: From Lubitsch to Sturges*, one salient fact remains for us to savor: "Comedy was Hollywood's essential genius."

*   *   *

Wilder's creative arc was rapidly developing, as was his ambition. Thanks to Goldwyn and now to Hawks, he was now permitted to be on set with Hawks while filming, and to witness at close range how "a non-idiot directed a motion picture," in his words. He hung around the set as much as he could for about ten weeks. Luckily for him, there wasn't much danger with Hawks of having clashes similar to those he'd had with Leisen. There might be other sorts of minor skirmishes, but nothing at all like the filmmaking nightmares he had barely survived.

But surprisingly, at least given my Stanwyck fetish as well as the quintessential performance she delivered, Miss Stanwyck was far from the first choice for the role, not even the second or third or fourth. Goldwyn wanted Ginger Rogers, who demurred by saying she preferred playing ladylike ladies; then he wanted Jean Arthur (another highly accomplished favorite comedic actress of mine), who liked the story but found Sugarpuss unsavory somehow; then Carole Lombard, who apparently liked the character but not the story. Lucille Ball was almost cast, until Cooper suggested Stanwyck, with whom he had previously worked on Capra's 1941 film *Meet John Doe*. Finally, Barbara was approached, loved it, and made it her own, cleverly realizing that the combination of Hawks at the helm with a gifted screenwriting team steering the snappy dialogue really couldn't be beat. So, she was more than ready to drum-boogie big-time.

Equally surprising—to me, at least—was Gary Cooper's well-known, if inexplicable, disdain for the writing of the story. Cooper was a highly competent Mr. Everyman actor, but by all accounts he was not, however, the sharpest knife in the drawer, and he made no secret of the fact that he hated the script, calling it "gibberish that doesn't make sense." This is surely as lame a response as Boyer not seeing the sheer pathos of having a prisoner be reduced to talking to a cockroach who couldn't answer back. Cooper also complained that he couldn't memorize the lines if they didn't mean anything. Goldwyn managed to convene a story conference to placate the star, after which he acquiesced and agreed to do the lines that had been crafted for him. Thank goodness, because language was at the heart of the tale, with its heartfelt take on a stodgy grammarian colliding with a streetwise babe in order to comprehend the idiomatic intricacies of popular and colloquial Yankee slang. Indeed, there were two kinds of language the writers wanted conveyed: the linguistic kind and the bawdy body language of Sugarpuss herself.

Even more impressive than what was accomplished on-screen was the behind-the-scenes fact that a mere seven years prior to embarking on this wisely dreamed-up cultural gem, Samuel "Billy" Wilder had arrived from Krakow speaking almost no English at all, at best haltingly and almost in an émigré slang picked up on the fly. Now, here he was extolling the virtues of proper communication between social classes for a work of cinematic art, a film crafted by a certified genius who was mentoring him in how to become a genius himself, or at least how to appear to be one. As for the language and writing skills themselves, they were of course the result of his early exposure to a patient tutor in the literary arts who taught him what actual Americans sounded like, all Americans, of every class: his gifted elder screenwriting collaborator, Charles Brackett.

When *Ball of Fire* was previewed in Sun Valley on October 29, it received fabulous acclaim and Goldwyn was delighted with the end result, leading Brackett and especially Wilder to imagine that the mogul would now naturally allow him to direct their next picture, a natural enough expectation. But Goldwyn was not known as a cautious and circumspect executive for nothing, and taking risks was not his forte. And as many have noted, from his perspective, Wilder was still not only *just* a writer, even if a very good one, he was also an abrasive know-it-all and a belligerent person all around. He was what Goldwyn called a "loose cannon," a talented but far too conceited artist who fought and screamed a lot. But still, Billy persisted stubbornly, remarking that "finally I pissed them off enough that they got rid of me by making me a director."

But even Brackett wasn't so sure if Wilder was capable of having the right directorial temperament, or of being able to restrain his own whims long enough, to venture into assembling a skilled team who *believed* strongly enough in him to devote a year or two of hard work to making those whims come true. After all, he was more than familiar with his volatile collaborator's penchant for striding around the office whacking his knee, and all the office furniture, with his riding crop as if he were already von Stroheim. Helen Hernandez, who was often called upon to be a referee during their frequent fights and screaming matches, was highly dubious about him, or them, being able to pull off such a feat.

Ed Sikov has accurately observed that the prospect of both collaborating on a screenplay and giving it to "the more volcanic of the two to direct . . . must have seemed lunatic." Indeed, and Brackett would have the added dread of not only completing an already difficult writing assignment but then serving as producer, and chief whipping boy, for a fellow writer with an already drastically inflated ego. From the corporate bosses' point of view, trusting an already notoriously wild writer to professionally handle all the subtle nuances and navigational dangers of an entire film project was a guaranteed recipe for disaster. The studio executives, as well as an army of Wilder's competitors and peers, many of whom he had already alienated, were relishing the prospect of seeing him get his comeuppance.

But as history has shown us all, the fact that he ascended to a lofty enough position to direct some twenty-four films after this first one proved that somehow he was right and they were, if not wrong, then at least misguided. Perhaps it was the crash course he had taken at the elbow of Howard Hawks, perhaps it was the forbearance of the long-suffering Brackett, perhaps it was mere good fortune, or perhaps a combination of all the above. Then again, it just may have been the case that he was, in fact, literally a born director, despite his own interpersonal flaws. And sure enough, as long as no homicides ensued, he could have a chance to have not the last laugh, but the first hurrah in a rather breathtaking, award-winning, and long-lasting career.

And so it was that following the example of the visionary Preston Sturges, their first independent venture as writer-director and writer-producer loomed. In the fall of 1941 work commenced and they had decided by November that the title would be *The Major and the Minor*, with a comfy comedic choice selected for their first outing, one that embraced a concept that was commercially viable and not too offensive—unless of course you find the notion of adult female star Ginger Rogers as a down-and-out woman who disguises herself as a twelve-year-old girl in order to qualify for a child's fare on a train, and then appear to be wooed by an adult Ray Milland who may or may not know of her clever ruse, somehow offensive? Either way, work on their first picture was persistently interrupted by reality: the attack on Pearl Harbor, blackouts, traffic stops, and a constant fear that possibly Los Angeles itself might be attacked.

Wilder's first debut as a director commenced in February 1942. Brackett barely concealed his amusement when he confided to his diary that editor Doane Harrison had told him that, when the fledgling director called out action, "his voice was a clear soprano." Wilder was securing more and more independence from the confines of their partnership, but the evolution of Brackett himself into a producer was almost accidental. The business deal for *The Major and the Minor* was structured so that Wilder, who had previously always been paid less than Brackett (the senior literary figure), was to be paid the same as his partner for both writing and for directing. That arrangement was not of course capable of being maintained, so Paramount stepped in and suggested that Brackett might start producing their films. Brackett viewed that corporate action, quite correctly, as only more unpaid work for himself. Perhaps it was even the kind of work for which he should have received an additional bonus, in the form of danger pay.

* * *

In actuality, the first film to be directed by Wilder was still produced by Arthur Hornblow Jr., a dependable choreographer of cinematic projects, with Brackett waiting for their next one to officially take the helm as associate producer, for which he would be very active in casting and preproduction issues, in addition to co-writing the script. It would take a while for both men to adjust to this fresh twist on their collaborations, and in some respects neither one ever really got used to this novel dynamic at all. But that still didn't stop them from forging forward and making great movies together. Indeed, they kept on keeping on—that is, up to the point where they just couldn't do it anymore.

The Major and the Minor was a transitional film, one that registered a major turning point for both men. Their professional relationship had always displayed cracks and fissures, but now, certain feelings started leaking out. And everyone knew it. The storyline, far-fetched by any standard, still had a certain risqué allure, and of course also had the requisite big stars bringing Brackett and Wilder's words to life. Paramount had optioned a play from 1923 called *Connie Goes Home*, with Ginger Rogers agreeing to play the lead character, whose name was changed to Susan Applegate, or Su-Su. Meanwhile costar Ray Milland had apparently been ambushed by Billy shouting from his car window on a corner of Melrose Avenue—"Would you work in a picture I'm going to direct?"—to which Ray had responded "Sure," noting later that "Hell, in those days you finished one picture on Friday and started a new one on Monday."

Ginger Rogers had recently won an Academy Award for Best Actress for *Kitty Foyle* and was at the time in a position of enough power to select her own director. Her agent—who also represented Wilder and Brackett—persuaded her to meet with still untried Wilder. She was open to the idea, and while she was filming *Roxie Hart*, they met at an Italian Restaurant to make and hear the pitch, with Ginger recalling later that Wilder, who must have been on his best behavior that day, was "charming, a real European gentleman . . . I've always been a good judge of character. I decided then and there that we would get along and that he had the qualities to become a good director. I felt that he would be strong, but that he would also listen. He certainly understood how to pay attention to a woman."

The offbeat project was ready to roll by January 1942. Its script tells the story of Susan Applegate, who, in a bind and broke, decides to impersonate a twelve-year-old girl so she can buy a cheaper train ticket as a minor. ("Is she a kid? Or is she kidding?" the film's sly publicity tag would ask.) On board, she meets Major Kirby (Milland), a military college instructor, whose fiancée, played by Rita Johnson, also shows up and reminds him, if only by her presence, who his intended really is. Kirby supposedly (though I'm not certain of this aspect at all) doesn't realize that Su-Su is a grown woman until the final scene of the farce. The Production Code Administration considered the entire project to be in bad taste. A week before filming commenced, the PCA declared to Paramount that many scenes were unacceptable, especially lines such as the double entendre delivered to Ginger earlier in the film by the great Robert Benchley before she needs to flee by train: "Why don't you get out of that wet coat and into a dry martini?"

The initial launch of Wilder into the directorial domain eventually worked out to everyone's satisfaction, even his own, and that was saying something. On February 23, Wilder's first day directing, Brackett wrote in his diary that "I went on the test stage and found him nervous but supported by Dr. Zinner and Doane Harrison. Nat Deverich suggested that, while Billy shoots I might take a job at RKO at a fantastically flattering price. Doubt that it could be obtained or that Paramount would want me to go." In any event, that potential moonlighting job fell through because Brackett wouldn't be able to assume it for about a month. So, he was still betrothed to Mr. Wilder for a while at least. Work on *The Major and the Minor* continued apace in their customary fashion: "A day of hell. Sniped away at the script with Billy absent on the set and at production meetings most of the time. Up early so I could be on set at 8:00 and watch the first shot, in Grand Central Station. It was so typical of Billy, whose element is tumult. He wasn't particularly nervous and one sees his confidence grow with the day."

But two days later, all hell broke loose, as usual. "I was working at RKO when a telephone call warned me of trouble on the set. I raced over to find Billy sweating in anguish. The scene that Ginger expected to be rewritten had not been rewritten. She just couldn't play it, she didn't understand it. Could Billy act it out for her?" Naturally, he acquiesced. The next day, back at the studio, Wilder appeared to be in good form, and they discussed the storyline. By June, as time roared ahead on multiple fronts, Brackett was agitated as he viewed a preview screening in Glendale. According to Brackett, "The man next to me was a wonderful audience, yelling with laughter, breathing with apprehension when the plot was tense. When the picture was over I turned to him and said, 'What did you think of it?' 'All right,' he replied."

In the midst of turmoil, Brackett was always able to rise above the tide and inject some slight bemusement into whatever was irking him, as for instance in July when the trade papers mentioned a rare personal event, the elopement of Brackett's daughter: "I was surprised. Expected them to read: Billy Wilder disturbed because of elopement of daughter of collaborator." Yet he was also facing daunting challenges in his professional relationship. "The team is in a bad way, over our heads, absolutely. We can't decide where we want to go. I am abysmally depressed." As always, though, his solution was to simply go with the tide, doing his best to bodysurf the tumult. Also as always, yet another picture loomed on the horizon, one that would be the exact opposite in tone to their inaugural Wilder-directed comedy.

Basically, the film, as surreal as the story sounds, worked so well due largely to a combination of Wilder's refusal to let censors control his work, and the exemplary ability of both Rogers and Milland to make the improbable seem reasonable. That and Wilder's additional moviemaking skills, already evident in his first outing. Rogers herself always maintained a soft spot for this quirky gem: "We had a lot of fun making the picture, and even though it was his first picture, from day one I saw that Billy knew what to do."

Reception for the film was wildly supportive, with the usually cranky Bosley Crowther of the *New York Times* admitting that the Brackett-Wilder script "effervesces with neat situations and bright lines. . . . The gentlemen have written—and Mr. Wilder has directed—a bountiful comedy-romance. And Miss Rogers and Mr. Milland have played it with spirit and with taste. Never once does either permit the suggestion of a leer to creep in."

This was an exceptional coup for the laid-back Ray Milland, a vastly underrated actor of consummate skill, charm, and grace, even more so perhaps because originally, Brackett and Wilder had crafted the role of Major Kirby with another actor in mind. *Variety* agreed with the overall accolades for all concerned, calling it "light, fluffy, and frolicsome. . . . Both script and direction swing the yarn along at a consistent pace, with the laughs developing naturally and without strain."

At his best, Wilder was always better than merely artistic, he was artful. In later years he also summed up his philosophy of invisible filmmaking quite succinctly: "When someone turns to his neighbor and says, 'My that was beautifully directed,' we have proof that it was not." His style of "cutting in the camera," learned at the elbow of Hawks and through night classes with his terrific editor Doane Harrison, called for a minimal amount of film to be shot; conscious, spontaneous editing decisions made during filming eliminated the need for, or danger of, studio heads later adding footage that the director deemed unnecessary. Billy summed up the approach this way: "When I finish a film, there is nothing left on the cutting room floor but chewing gum wrappers and tears." An apt description, and one that explains Wilder's use of Harrison's services for every subsequent film all the way through *The Fortune Cookie* (1966).

Most importantly, for the studio which was expecting him to fail, or almost hoping he would, Wilder completed the film almost exactly within his allotted budget, something that pleased them greatly. This achievement, even more than the accolades about the venture, pretty much assured him the opportunity of getting another film to direct. And that would be the first one to be produced solely by Brackett. They were also in agreement that having accomplished a lighthearted and farcical fantasy that the public had relished, the next one could be something far heavier, something with which they could hit audiences over the head emotionally.

PART TWO

TRAGEDY

We actually participate in a tragedy, while at a comedy we only watch it.

ALDOUS HUXLEY

CHAPTER FIVE

ONWARD AND DOWNWARD

Something Wicked This Way Comes

A wedge of sunlight slipped over the edge of the desk and fell noiselessly to the carpet.

RAYMOND CHANDLER

The partners first pitched their next film to Paramount executive Buddy DeSylva, sharing their notions and getting his approval, but also his urgent request for a title—"So urgent that my mind dried up at once," Brackett wrote. Four days later however, they settled on the title, *Five Graves to Cairo*. DeSylva's response was tepid at first: he didn't like it, fearing that the word "graves" would keep people away from theaters. But by the end of that conference he had accepted the title. Things change rapidly in Tinseltown. DeSylva was not the only executive to have problems with the title. One office hack suggested "Five to Cairo," which the screenwriting team disregarded as meaningless. Another tried to impose "Rommel's Last Stand," an equally inane title which Brackett and Wilder rejected "as poor a title ever suggested for anything and completely inappropriate for this film. Take our word for it: we would have nothing to do with any picture so baptized."

By August 13, they were in gear, producing three pages of the script: "good, grim pages," in Brackett's words. He and Wilder were on the cusp of writing, producing, and directing some of the darkest and most disturbing films in Hollywood history. Ever versatile, though, while Wilder was busy shooting tests of Franchot Tone, Brackett took the breather as an opportunity to work on a script all his own, *The Uninvited*, a pleasantly distracting ghost story he would produce starring Ray Milland a couple of years down the road, while Wilder was struggling with Brackett's temporary "replacement," Raymond Chandler, in the writing and directing of one of the greatest noir masterpieces ever made.

By October, some of the cracks in their mutual armor appeared to become more obvious, revolving primarily around *The Uninvited*, but only as a triggering device. In his diary, Brackett wrote, "Billy and I are in disagreement because I think Jacques Thery should be employed as a story advisor, both on *Five Graves* and *The Uninvited*. Billy wants him on *The Uninvited* only . . . and I feel that generous as he is to most people about credit, he is extraordinarily mean to Jacques, who really helps him more than anyone."

I believe this lays bare part of the toxicity that had set in to the already slightly rancid relationship the two men had: *The Uninvited* was a Brackett picture intended to launch Charlie as an independent producer, one occasionally freed from Billy's long shadow. Only incidentally did it overlap with the noir classic-to-be, *Double Indemnity*, that Billy was then cooking up, one which sent a chill up and down the spine of the redemption-loving Republican Brackett, and which he was quite pleased to dissociate himself from. Let the rot settle into someone else's soul for a change, he may have surmised at 3:00 in the morning one day, and he would gladly leave the whole deal in the trembling fingers of Mr. Chandler, whose soul might already be beyond repair anyway.

By November 1942, the strange pressures of producing *Five Graves* seemed to be getting the better of Brackett: "A session with DeSylva in which Billy got him to consent to Anne Baxter as leading lady—as dreary a little piece as I ever saw. . . . Tonight I am playing with the thought, ecstatically, of casting off the utterly foolish pretense that I am producing *Five Graves to Cairo* and going back to my office on the fourth floor." By December 16, things were coming to a head, although weren't they always? "There are times when I look at Billy, the best dramatic mind with which I ever came in contact, with the appalling feeling that his mind is dropping apart before my eyes—its brilliant decisiveness crumbling to utterly foolish indecisions."

Having carefully crafted an amusing, crowd-pleasing, daffy appetizer for their opening salvo, Brackett and Wilder were now fully prepared to deliver a whole new menu, with a main course that took a drastic detour away from the style and sensibility they were best known for. Their last message, sent special delivery in *The Major and the Minor*, their first fully controlled project, was basically: You know us, you know what we do best, and we have no interest in pulling any fast ones on our loyal audience. But with the ominously titled *Five Graves to Cairo*, their message was equally simple but also drastically divergent: You don't know us, you have no idea what we do best, and we're going to pull the rug out from under you both stylistically and thematically, in a brutal way you'll never forget. Get ready for our tragedies, they seemed to be declaring: straight up, no chaser.

In casting the movie, Wilder had originally wanted, and approached, Cary Grant to play the role that eventually went to Franchot Tone, who did a fine job as Corporal Bramble. David Selznick had agreed to lend Ingrid Bergman to appear in this second Wilder feature, but instead, for unclear reasons, Paramount borrowed Anne Baxter from Twentieth Century Fox for the role of Mouche. I've always been glad that Grant and Bergman were not featured as initially hoped for by Wilder, since they would have drained all the acting oxygen out of the script with their star power.

Brackett and Wilder were formally assigned to *Five Graves* on August 10, 1942, in what must have felt like the blink of a screenwriter's eye after their whimsical train trip with Ginger. Continuing their proven track record as writing partners, although never happy ones, they jointly assembled the plot structure and character development. As usual, Brackett was the physical writer of the draft pages, while Wilder barked complaints and commands, until Brackett then handed it off to Helen Hernandez to be typed, if she could read it.

When the coauthors began to write the blueprint for *Five Graves*, the battle for North Africa was still raging, with Nazis and their fascist Italian counterparts pummeling the British all across the Egyptian desert. This current affairs aspect was striking and gave the film a weirdly documentary feel. While their writing continued intensely in the fall of 1942, global military events seemed to take a turn for the better. And the notorious Field Marshal Erwin German Rommel (who would be played in the film to mesmerizing menacing effect by Erich von Stroheim) made some surprising tactical errors as the Americans and British launched fresh offensive campaigns. Rommel tried to finally take El-Alamein, but his weary troops were not up to the task, forcing him to undertake a full retreat. Hitler ordered him to stay in place and continue to fight a hopeless fight, but Rommel placed himself in clear peril by disregarding his leader's direct command and shifting his troops seven hundred miles away near a little Libyan port called Benghazi. That retreat would be one of the first clear Allied victories in the war up to that point.

From the perspective of two screenwriters feeding on actual reality for their storyline, the prospects looked affirming enough and they plunged ahead with a shimmering and hard-edged script. Meanwhile, as they were absorbed in a considerably more noirish frame of mind for their wartime epic (in quiet emotive power, if not in explosive scale), *The Major and the Minor* was soaring at the box office in a record-breaking five-week-long run.

Eventual production would last from January 4 to February 20, 1943, and filming took place at Paramount Studios in Hollywood with a few exterior shots conducted on location at Salton Sea and Camp Young, the Army Desert Training Centre, which helped them stage several battle scenes in Indio, California as well as Yuma, Arizona. But although the film was clearly an elegiac wartime drama with vivid military overtones, it was also, and in keeping with the Brackett-Wilder modus operandi of probing underlying intimacies, still a personal story of love, hate, intrigue, and private loss. Corporal Bramble, the Franchot Tone character, is the sole survivor of a British tank crew after Rommel's capture of the city of Tobruk. He wanders across the desert until he comes upon a tiny and nearly deserted hotel owned by one Farid, assisted by a French chambermaid, Anne Baxter's character, named Mouche.

Farid hides the barely conscious Bramble when the advancing Germans take over the hotel to use as a headquarters, then, once regaining his senses, Bramble impersonates a dead hotel waiter in order to save himself from Rommel, who proceeds to reveal that Davos, the real waiter, was also an esteemed German spy. Bramble has no choice but to play along and try to survive, and is ordered by Rommel to travel to Cairo. While listening to the depraved Field Marshal toying with his "guests," Bramble learns that Rommel has secretly prepared five hidden supply and weapons dumps that he plans to use for the conquest of Egypt. These are, in fact, the "Five Graves" in the film's title. Bramble's information, and his clever detection of their locations from the ceaseless sinister banter of Rommel, aids the British in blowing up the "graves," which culminates in the second Battle of El-Alamein.

When the corporal finally returns to the bleak hotel, thinking he will be celebrating both his own and the Allies' triumph, he discovers that the Germans have executed Mouche for bravely declaiming that the British would be back to eliminate Rommel and his kind from the planet. This sorrowful aspect still permitted the use of a classic Brackett and Wilder promo tagline, "Did a woman start the rout of Rommel?" Bramble mournfully takes the parasol he purchased as a gift for her in Cairo—something she had always dreamed of having—and uses it to provide shade over her grave. Rommel was indeed routed, but the impactful image of sheer sadistic evil left on the screen by the brilliant von Stroheim, who practically steals the whole movie, has remained a permanent part of the lore surrounding stellar supporting character roles.

The meeting between the charismatic and nutty von Stroheim and his director Billy Wilder carried with it undertones for both men. As a young Berlin-based journalist, Wilder had written a memorable profile piece for the art magazine *Der Querschnitt*, "Stroheim, the man you love to hate," another snappy line that further revealed his uncanny skill with the aesthetics of advertising. "It's especially Stroheim who, in my youth, struck me," Wilder later explained. "My ideal, if the mix is possible, would be Lubitsch plus Stroheim." He meant by this odd combination something celebrating gritty realism, elegant wit, gorgeous cinematography, and a swiftly flowing screenplay. It was not only possible; Wilder would actually accomplish this fanciful feat in this and several of his upcoming pictures, such as *The Lost Weekend*, *Double Indemnity* (the film Brackett would not work on), and, most importantly, in the vast stylistic perfection of *Sunset Boulevard*, which also karmically featured von Stroheim again, pretty much playing himself, again, but doing it brilliantly.

Unbelievably, Paramount remained convinced that, if the writer-producer and writer-director were allowed to indulge what they misunderstood to be flagrant whims, their investment would be doomed. As late as January, with filming wrapping up, their studio bosses made the eccentric decision to hold a series of publicity contests designed to generate more suitable titles for their movie.

Obviously they had been unable to do that themselves, and being crass businessmen at heart, they deduced that letting the public decide would be the best arrangement. It wasn't. Some of the semi-finalists were truly lame, including "North Africa," "Appointment in Africa," "Hellfire Pass," "Afrika Korps," "Africa Aflame," "Desert Fury," "Beyond the Line of Duty," and "One Came Back."

All of them—with the possible exception of that last one, which has a certain charm—were dead on arrival, so much so that the letter sent from the executives to Brackett and Wilder requesting their opinions or approvals went loudly disregarded. Mostly that was because *Five Graves to Cairo* is a perfect title, capturing as it does the essence of something gritty but alluring at the same time, a hallmark of Wilder ever after. It was a phenomenon crafted out of Wilder's complex character and unusual artistic skills, to be sure. The public clearly loved both emotional seasonings, and their wartime saga likewise succeeded at the box office.

Perhaps it was the fervid sprinkling of a little patriotic spice, as exemplified by Bramble's final soliloquy at Mouche's graveside: "Don't worry, Mouche. We're after them now. When you feel the earth shake, that'll be our tanks and our guns. Thousands and thousands of them—British, French, and American. We're after them now, coming from all sides. We're going to blast the blazes out of them." Without consciously striving to do so, the film's makers had introduced, through the lens of national combat, a style capable of also conveying the richly tense paradoxes of personal and domestic combat. It was a pristine aesthetic and an icy emotional style of highly visual storytelling that came to be identified with their work through the mid to late forties and up to their final parting. Brackett and Wilder, both together and apart, would very soon submit for our dreadful edification some of the finest examples of sheer noir genius in cinematic history.

*   *   *

Melodrama: the essential link between classical tragedy and "dark film." "Suffering, with style" was the succinct and totally apt way that Turner Classic Movies curator Eddie Muller chose to characterize the unique mode of film noir storytelling. "The men and women of this sinister cinematic world are driven by greed, lust, jealousy, and revenge, which leads inexorably to existential torment, soul-crushing despair, and a few last gasping breaths in a rain-soaked gutter. But damned if these lost souls don't look sensational riding the Hades Express. If you're going straight to hell, you might as well travel with some style to burn."

From the moment the term *film noir*—dark film—was first conceived by advanced French critics in the postwar global culture, there was also an instant debate about what it encapsulated so vividly. Muller, who is also an author of crime fiction himself, further defines the concept as one about a certain kind of people—a protagonist who, driven to act out of some desperate desire, does something that he or she knows to be wrong, even knowing what dire consequences will follow. Karma always looms large in noir. And monumentally so in the noir classics created by Brackett and Wilder, who would approach the genre in subversive ways that first enlivened and then more or less obliterated moral cinema codes altogether.

In addition to homegrown American stylists, of course, the other major source of suffering, in style, would be the many film directors who fled Nazi Germany, both to survive literally and also to thrive artistically, and they brought with them a heightened visual signature style that essentially was derived from the German Expressionist movement. Fritz Lang, Otto Preminger, Robert Siodmak, Curtis Bernhardt, and of course Wilder, tended to carry the darkness they had just escaped in their hearts, and they gleefully shared it with the rest of us. As Muller characterizes the crossbreeding, it was largely the character-focus that shifted: "What made these films popular with the American public was the newfound willingness—even eagerness—of major stars to play amoral characters. Bogart set the tone. Plenty of imitations followed, characters with a savvy attitude and a smart mouth, and when they tumbled off the fence to the dark side, you had a truly noir protagonist."

This sudden turn toward the dark was fueled by a postwar appetite for bad people doing bad things, and most surprisingly of all, many of the actors and actresses who had built substantial careers on their signature images of good, cute, kind, humane roles, now were matched with directors who wanted to show a more human, if less humane, side of our natures. The best example of this shift would naturally be both Fred MacMurray and Barbara Stanwyck, he a lightweight comedic actor of great skill and her a charming lighthearted girl-next-door type. But when the visionary Billy Wilder chose them both to play against type in his classic noir *Double Indemnity*, something that made Stanwyck quite nervous, he was also inviting them to take a chance that might or might not threaten their commercial popularity.

Not only did it not damage either of them professionally at all, instead it was the key to launching them both into a whole other dimension of their acting craft, and one that the public adored. If not for that latter career phase, we might not remember either of them quite so vividly. Describing some of the idealized beauty, snappy dialogue, and quick-witted behaviors of the greatest noir performances, Muller summed up our fondness for these usually unsavory folks very well: "If only we could all think this fast and look this good. In the final analysis, that probably sums up noir's eternal appeal as well as anything. Today, the cynicism and fatalism found in classic noir seems almost comforting compared to the pessimism we confront on movie screens."

For me, the most effective evocation of the noir sensibility and its origins in ancient tragedy via melodrama was explored by Robert

Kolker in his *Film, Form, and Culture*, a book that never stops clarifying our often obscure modernist connections to antiquity. In it, he also reminds us that the malleability of documentary films (even those so extreme as to use actual footage of atrocities) always seems to be greater than the fiction film genres, which appear to be more bound by the obvious rules and conventions self-imposed early on in the history of film. Most importantly, he points out that genres are such complex things that focusing on just two, melodrama and noir, demonstrates for us how their structures, themes, and variations work:

> One of the genres, melodrama, is very old and predates cinema, the other one, noir, is relatively new and particular to film. Melodrama can be understood as a genre and a master narrative, an overarching narrative form that controls all films that aren't comedies and that had an existence before film was invented. Film noir, on the other hand, is original to film and is also a kind of hybrid. It developed out of detective fiction, the gangster film, thirties French cinema, the thriller, and melodrama itself. Curiously, at the time of the creation of noir in the early forties, nobody knew that they were inventing what would become one of the most celebrated of all genres.

There is, of course, a direct cinematic line that can be traced from Welles's *Citizen Kane* in 1941, through *Double Indemnity* in 1944 and *The Lost Weekend* in 1945, and culminating with stunning brilliance in *Sunset Boulevard* in 1950.

* * *

Around this time, Brackett felt that he had two choices: to continue his present course, a life "buffered against the difficulties of Hollywood by Billy Wilder, or to end our association, without animosity but in exhaustion." In October 1942, Brackett had commenced work on associate-producing *The Uninvited*, a fairly lighthearted ghost story to be written by Dodie Smith in tandem with another of Brackett's earlier collaborators, Frank Patros. He was bothered big-time when in January 1943, while the shooting of *Five Graves* was still going on, the *Hollywood Reporter* printed a mistaken, or accidental, piece saying that Wilder would be directing *The Uninvited*, an error that greatly riled Brackett and necessitated a correction statement. At that point, Wilder too started searching for projects he could do without Brackett.

As Brackett wrote in his diary, "In Billy's manner there is a carefully groomed suggestion of the brush-off. And why the hell shouldn't he brush me off. He's done the major part of our work for the past three years, and the fact that I made considerable sacrifices to get him his director's job has been amply repaid. Also I am happy in the belief that, while not as good without Billy, I'm pretty good—and more self-respecting." But, why *not* be brushed off? Really? Well for one thing, Brackett still had the glistening brilliance of both *The Lost Weekend* and *Sunset Boulevard to* contribute—well worth the effort, as I see it.

Regarding the causes of the temporary split-up between the ambitious young director and his senior writer-producer partner while contemplating *Double Indemnity*, one school of thought has it that although this film represented the first serious blow to both their collaborative partnership and personal relationship, by 1942 Brackett had already decided that if he were to be forced into a parallel role of producer then he might as well make the best of it and actually produce something without Wilder as well.

On March 11, the real crux of their crisis became more obvious: "Billy got a telephone call and consulted me about *Double Indemnity*, a story Joe Sistrom suggested to him which he wants to do, not leaving Joe out. I got the hint and talked it over with Leland and we decided Billy was having a touch of claustrophobia at being tied down to working with me, so I told him to go ahead with Joe. Buddy DeSylva nixed it, saying we should stay together." In the meantime, Brackett distracted himself with work on the script and production of *The Uninvited*, whose first day of shooting was April 15.

Unfortunately, his attempt to distract himself in an independent project had some unforeseen consequences at the other end of the conference table. On May 10, Brackett observed that "I find the pleasure I have been taking in *The Uninvited* has been completely poisoned by Billy's return, and my pleasure in life as well." Two weeks later an attempt was made to put some distance between himself and the younger cranky genius, as Brackett told Wilder he intended to get a different office, a move that Wilder objected to. By June, Wilder had commenced the actual writing on *Double Indemnity*, although he had yet to decide on the male lead actor.

Originally, Wilder had planned to direct a snappy musical as the follow-up to his war picture, but while dreaming it up he was stopped in his tracks by a competing movie and a very good one, *Cover Girl*. "I realized that no matter how good my musical would be most people would say it was no *Cover Girl*. So this *Double Indemnity* looked like a better chance to set Hollywood back on its heels." As has often been observed, to make this film work, given its disturbing antihero/antiheroine matchup, would require the skillful juggling of paradoxical impulses in the audience, requiring an almost impossible balance of cinematic finesse and a human treatment of the inhuman characters caught in the throes of their vulgar compulsions.

Double Indemnity has gone down in Hollywood history as one that Brackett detested as distastefully unsavory and, after initially trying, refused to ultimately write the screenplay for. Nonetheless, Brackett still wrote the initial treatment for it with Wilder, and joined story meetings with Wilder and the script's co-writer, Raymond Chandler. Even if he didn't want to finish the writing aspect he still seems to have been prepared to produce it. Yet it wasn't so much the sordid nature of the sinister characters that turned Brackett off, though he did dislike them intensely; it was more that their darkness was unrelenting and led to no redemption. Brackett didn't mind cruelty or selfishness in strong-willed characters, evident from the fact that he would return to Wilder the following year to write the despair derby of *The Lost Weekend*, but he also craved punishment and justice too—and, if at all possible, redemption.

Luckily for both men, Brackett's temporary writing replacement, the perennially plastered Raymond Chandler, although an able and proven novelist and sinister storyteller, was a person for whom Wilder quickly developed an undiluted hatred. Collaborative stresses were not new to him of course, since the Brackett and Wilder working method—screaming, fighting, storming off, and returning again to the job at hand—had inadvertently created a uniquely powerful bond between them, maybe even a warped kind of love.

But in the case of Chandler, who nevertheless handed in a serviceable and very Chandler-like script, it was all warp, with zero love, or even respect. He claimed that his exposure to this "volatile, bullheaded foreigner who couldn't stop pacing" left him physically and emotional exhausted. Writing to his British publisher Hamish Hamilton, Chandler declared defiantly that "Working with Billy Wilder was an agonizing experience and has probably shortened my life." He later followed up the assessment with an unnamed set of targets in a vitriolic screed against Hollywood: "The pretentiousness, the bogus enthusiasm, the constant drinking and drabbing, the incessant squabbling over money, the all-pervasive agent, the strutting of the big shots (and their usually utter incompetence to achieve anything they set out to do), the constant fear of losing all this fairy gold and being the nothing they have never ceased to be, the snide tricks, the whole damn mess is out of this world." All of that might have been accurate. In fact, most Hollywood insiders would recognize Chandler's weather report as just daily life, and some of them, such as Wilder, were actually able to thrive in that very combustible echo chamber.

And just as Wilder always knew how good his own work was, he likewise knew how good *Double Indemnity* was, despite its many challenges to life and limb. He was totally serious when he arrived on set one day and demanded complete silence: "Keep it quiet! After all, history is being made here!" And so it was. Later on, while watching the rushes for *Double Indemnity*, Brackett would be unable to conceal his decided disdain, saying that he found them a little monotonous in their single note of brutality. (It should be stated that when he saw the final cut version of *Double Indemnity*, Brackett relented and exclaimed that it was brilliant, an "absolute knockout.")

Double Indemnity was an example of a dictum detected by Charlotte Chandler in her late, end-of-career talks with Wilder: "Billy Wilder lived by his wits, and his characters often lived by theirs. Sometimes they died by their wits." Wilder often downplayed the aesthetics of his craft, avoiding artsy explanations of how or why he did what he did, in favor of more seemingly self-effacing approaches: "The main characters in *Double Indemnity* have a problem. They aren't living the American dream, and they hope to correct that. The game is as important as the gain. I just made the pictures I would have liked to see myself. When I was lucky, it coincided with the taste of the audience. With *Double Indemnity*, I was very lucky."

Paul Schrader, as both a filmmaker and a historian, has always been the most reliable appreciator of what made noir noirish. He has described *Double Indemnity* as "the best-written, the most characteristically film noir of the period. *Double Indemnity* was the first film which played film noir for what it was: small-time, undreamed, unheroic."

The novella on which the film is based itself drew on an actual 1927 murder perpetrated by a Queens, New York, woman and her lover, whose trial author James Cain attended while working as a journalist. The story started circulating around Hollywood in 1936, the year Cain became famous for his novel *The Postman Always Rings Twice*, published the year before. Studios were wary due to the vibe of the story, similar in many ways to that enacted on-screen by John Garfield and Lana Turner in *The Postman*. Indeed, the storyline was one that Hollywood had long thought to be unfilmable. The censors found no redeeming merits to the project: "The general low tone and sordid flavor of this story makes it, in our judgment, thoroughly unacceptable for screen presentation before mixed audiences. It is most important to avoid 'the hardening of audiences' to the thought and fact of crime."

Double Indemnity is an absolute masterpiece, quite rightly considered a landmark in the noir style trend that most accurately commenced with the opulently visual gem of *Citizen Kane* by Orson Welles three years earlier. Beyond its visual dimension, journalist Robert Kolker has pointed out that it was the structure of the dialogue and the deadpan narration in the film that truly made a mark: "It synthesized noir's essential generic elements—bitter ironic dialogue, a weak male character who falls prey to a female predator, and a mise-en-scène unrelentingly gray and claustrophobic. The streets add to the pervading atmosphere of limited sleazy lives." Observing that there is as little sentimentality in this film as Hollywood could allow, Kolker also was astute enough to catch the inherent paradox at the heart of this acidic ode, the fact that it can be read in two ways, like all great art. It is "either a misogynist film about a terrifying, destroying woman, or it a film that liberates the female character from the restrictive and oppressed melodramatic situations that render her helpless. Feminist critics are divided in their views of the film and the noir genre as a whole." The core sensibility of early noir was already present in *Five Graves*, but it may have been lost on some viewers since the setting was a desert and not a rainy urban street. But all the hallmarks were already there, waiting for the right moment to emerge.

In Hollywood circles it was widely believed that both men secretly hoped that the other would fail without their collaboration. Both were wrong on that count too, with Wilder's new noir being an instant classic, and Brackett's ghost story being rather well received. Wilder, perhaps bugged that his partner was being praised without him, bestowed his typically cynical form of Billy-accolade: "You cheated on me! I expected you to come back with a social disease—instead, you come back with a baby!"

Nonetheless, Billy and Charlie managed to patch things up more or less to the satisfaction of each side of their boiling creative equation. Wilder's next chosen project would be another darkly disturbing movie, but this time focusing on a laboriously slow self-destruction. If Wilder thought he had been "lucky" with the brilliantly dank *Double Indemnity*—which was nominated for seven Oscars, including Best Picture and Best Director, but which won nothing—he would surely hit the mother lode with his next film, *The Lost Weekend*.

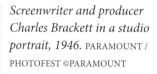

Screenwriter and producer
Charles Brackett in a studio
portrait, 1946. PARAMOUNT /
PHOTOFEST ©PARAMOUNT

Screenwriter and director Billy
Wilder in a studio portrait,
1946. PARAMOUNT / PHOTOFEST
©PARAMOUNT

Brackett and Wilder with
director Mitchell Leisen,
working on Midnight, 1939.
PARAMOUNT / PHOTOFEST
©PARAMOUNT

Brackett and Wilder with Claudette Colbert during the making of Arise My Love, *1940.* PARAMOUNT / PHOTOFEST ©PARAMOUNT

Brackett and Wilder engaged in their usual struggle during the writing of The Major and the Minor, *1942.* PARAMOUNT / PHOTOFEST ©PARAMOUNT

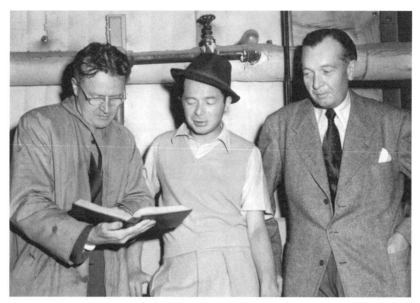

Brackett and Wilder with their trusted editor Doane Harrison, conferring over a script. HISTORIC COLLECTION / ALAMY STOCK PHOTO

Fred MacMurray toying with Barbara Stanwyck in Double Indemnity, *1944.*
PARAMOUNT / PHOTOFEST ©PARAMOUNT

Howard da Silva tries to dissuade star Ray Milland from drinking in The Lost Weekend, *1945.* PARAMOUNT / PHOTOFEST ©PARAMOUNT

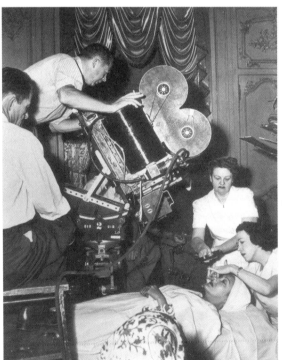

Wilder directing Gloria Swanson in her infamous bed scene for Sunset Boulevard, *1950.* PARAMOUNT / PHOTOFEST ©PARAMOUNT

Wilder demonstrating for Goria Swanson how to be crazy, for Sunset Boulevard.

Charles Brackett, Gloria Swanson, and Billy Wilder pretending to be friendly during the making of Sunset Boulevard, *1949.*

The captivating publicity poster for Sunset Boulevard *("A Hollywood Story"), a film noir masterpiece.* PARAMOUNT / PHOTOFEST ©PARAMOUNT

William Holden, the troubled writer in Sunset Boulevard. PARAMOUNT / PHOTOFEST ©PARAMOUNT

Writer Joe Gillis is forced by a crazed Norma Desmond to watch her legendary old movies. PARAMOUNT / PHOTOFEST ©PARAMOUNT

Swanson descends the staircase in the distressing final scene of Sunset Boulevard. PARAMOUNT / PHOTOFEST ©PARAMOUNT

Kirk Douglas tries to shed light on one of the darkest of film noirs, Ace in the Hole, *1951, the first film Wilder created on his own after his divorce from Brackett.* PARAMOUNT / PHOTOFEST ©PARAMOUNT

The King and I, *with Deborah Kerr and Yul Brynner, 1956. Perhaps the greatest hit that Charles Brackett created as a solo producer, after his divorce from Wilder.* PARAMOUNT / PHOTOFEST ©PARAMOUNT

CHAPTER SIX

TEA FOR TWO

One's Company, Two's a Crowd

It's like the doctor was just telling me—delirium is a disease of the night. Good night.

NURSE BIM, IN *THE LOST WEEKEND*

Years later, long after he had more or less successfully convinced himself that he was the sole driving force in his partnership with Brackett, Wilder was interviewed by Garson Kanin, and he couched their collaboration in strangely domestic terms, almost as a kind of professional adultery: "1944 was The Year of Infidelities. Charlie produced *The Uninvited*. I had nothing to do with it. I wrote *Double Indemnity* with Raymond Chandler . . . and I don't think he ever forgave me. He always thought I cheated on him with Raymond Chandler. He got very possessive after that." Not too surprisingly, Brackett had a different take on the turn of events, telling the same interviewer that "Billy got so despondent about being without me that I did *Lost Weekend* with him, a depressing film about an alcoholic writer who has trouble writing."

As Anthony Slide, editor of Brackett's diaries, has noted, in 1944, Brackett and Wilder were involved in a "quite confusing" array of different film projects, some of them abandoned. This seems to be indicative of a team that is flailing about, trying to tread water with each using the other to hold themselves afloat without pulling both of them down. By May 3, 1944, the two were being interviewed by Lincoln Barnett for an famous/infamous profile in *Life* as "The Happiest Couple in Hollywood," which would appear in the December 11 issue. The next day, after working in the morning, they met with novelist Charles Jackson for lunch at Romanoff's. His first novel, *The Lost Weekend*, published that year, would prove to be the vehicle that reunited Brackett and Wilder, and would win them an Academy Award the following year.

Still, the chasm continued to widen, with Brackett observing one day in August, "Billy hurried away. I asked him what was up. He said that they had figured it out that to get the most out of us there must be one picture together, then one apart—like *Double Indemnity* and *The Uninvited*. Went home depressed, though I've long felt that a parting of the ways was inevitable. Sorry it has to happen when Billy is in so entirely agreeable a mood." Such agreeability, however, was always very short-lived.

If nothing else, their separate vacations away from their usual collaborative routine did result in two very important occurrences: First, the creation of a Wilder masterpiece in *Double Indemnity*, which had the corollary impact of showing them both just how much their joint magic depended on their other half. Second, the breather also firmly cemented their awareness of how important great screenplays were to making great movies, and a deep love of words and taut writing was for them the key to any film's success. Their belief that language was essential to cinema was now even more clearly an ethic that they shared going forward. The smartest artists working in Hollywood all knew the crucial value of both a finely crafted screenplay and also the interactive give-and-take relationship between a great producer and gifted director.

This has been a rich area for research and scholarship, with James Park's short book *Learning to Dream*, on the new British cinema, taking a forceful approach to appreciating these working relationships between art and commerce. According to Park, "The director plays a central role in the creation of a stylistically coherent and visually interesting film, but the contributions of many people are essential. The main concern for the new directors is to find ways to become more effective by maximizing the potential of all the collaborators in a film project." And one of the core techniques for maximizing that potential is to learn to find a way not to kill your chief collaborator. While still tense after their trial separation, both Brackett and Wilder were willing to overlook personal slights in order to achieve their shared objective, especially with a piece of work as riveting as *The Lost Weekend*.

For postmodern film masters like Jean-Luc Godard, "The script is essentially made for the financiers. It has nothing to do with filmmaking but is merely a convenient way of showing a producer how the money is being spent." In Brackett and Wilder's case, however, since one of the writers in their team was also a producer, there was a decided bonus to having him be as cognizant and appreciative of the language as the director, who in their case was also chiefly a writer at heart. It's yet another aspect of their dynamic, factoring into the overall forward flow of their adaptation of Charles Jackson's story a personal component, one where the life-experience parallels are evident in their approach to making it. Believing as I do that the best designation for film noir is that of *decadent melancholia*, *The Lost Weekend* was therefore the perfect narrative vehicle for both men to explore its depths.

The biographer Axel Madsen observed that *The Lost Weekend*'s "vision of New York remains the most unsparing ever recorded on film. Here is a nightmare of litter-strewn streets, a cluttered apartment looking onto a desolate cityscape, the elevated train clanging up Third Avenue in the dirty light of a summer morning." Yet Pauline Kael had unreserved feelings, not only about *The Lost Weekend*, but also, almost inexplicably, about what she perceived or imagined to be images and stories indicative of the "distinctive cruel edge" which she personally identified as the specialist domain of the Brackett-Wilder writing team.

Numerous critics and writers have argued that the personal lives of the film's writers were reflected in their adaptation of the dismal nightmare that haunts *The Lost Weekend*'s Don Birnam, the troubled writer played so powerfully and believably by Ray Milland. Matthew Dessem has pointed out the many alcoholics in Brackett's family, including his wife and daughter, as well as the drunks he encountered at the Algonquin Round Table. Wilder biographer Maurice Zolotow has argued, "It is evident to me, that Brackett was writing himself in the characters of Don Birnam's brother and Jane Wyman, and that Wilder was writing Wilder in the opposing constellation of sardonic characters—Howard da Silva's bartender, Doris Dowling's hooker, Frank Faylen's homosexual Bellevue Hospital nurse." Ed Sikov, on the other hand, while finding some appeal in Zolotow's interpretations, has gone even further into the hyper-personal underpinnings there in the film for all to see: "*The Lost Weekend*'s appeal to the two screenwriters was much simpler and also more complicated. Both Brackett and Wilder *were* Don Birnam. They were writers after all, and while neither Brackett nor Wilder was a terminal drunk, they each bore a familiar burden of self-contempt—familiar to writers, anyway." It also must have been equally sobering to get to write and direct this particular follow-up to *Double Indemnity*, which Wilder had co-written under hideous circumstances, coping with the challenges of a periodically zonked-out or entirely absent lushy novelist. Chandler had been a recovering alcoholic during that stint and claimed that the stress and tumult of his working relationship with Wilder (actually not that much different from Wilder's relationship with Brackett) caused him to start drinking again to survive the collaboration. Wilder has claimed that he made the film, at least partly, in order to explain Chandler to himself.

For Brackett's part, he also had the distant memory of his own friendships with expatriate Yanks in Europe—heavy, self-destructive drinkers such as Fitzgerald and Hemingway, among others—which he had profiled vividly in his early novel *American Colony*. More recently, there was of course Charlie's first wife, Elizabeth Fletcher Brackett, a reclusive perpetual drinker whom he had to institutionalize once, but to no avail. He also had another private interest in the Charles Jackson novel, and his adaptive screenplay for it, in the form of that author's distressing but powerful portrayal of a seriously closeted gay man. Don Birnam's primary motive in his drinking was to dull the pain of his own true identity. In this context, it has been widely reported that Brackett often tried to secure acting jobs for his son-in-law James Larmore—in many accounts, his secret lover—for a little character role in *The Lost Weekend*.

But Wilder had a serious allergy to Larmore, seeing in him, quite accurately, just another unreliable drunk himself. Wilder apparently stopped going to the Bracketts' dinners on Sunday because he dreaded running into him. For his part, Brackett could never understand Wilder's reluctance to help an acquaintance out with a small role, and he observed that Billy often extended such boons to his own girlfriends. Either way, their work continued apace and with the usual ups and downs, progressing well through the summer of 1944, except of course for the usual squawking from the Hays censorship office about ill-advised or unsavory subject matter, which pretty much comprised the script in its entirety.

Originally Wilder wanted José Ferrer for the role of the alcoholic writer but that actor declined, possibly due to how unflattering the portrayal would be. His first choice for the female lead, Olivia de Havilland, also had to decline due to contractual agreements preventing her taking on new work. Most of the film was shot at the

Paramount studios in Hollywood, but Wilder also insisted that a sense of realism would be achieved by location-shooting in New York, including the notorious alcoholic ward of Bellevue Mental Hospital. Once the film was finished and shown to preview audiences, Wilder was appalled to discover that viewers were laughing (at first) at the intense and overwrought emotional pitch of Ray Milland's performance.

Paramount even considered canning the film entirely, after a concerted public relations campaign and open letter from the liquor industry objecting to its tone, an attempt to undermine its release by outrageously claiming that the picture would inspire anti-drinking groups to reinstate Prohibition. Legend has it that the liquor industry even sought the help of notorious gangster Frank Costello to offer Paramount five million dollars to sell the negative so it could be destroyed. The film was placed temporarily on the shelf by unimaginative executives who were always afraid too of much reality in "their pictures," and took far too seriously the reactions of preview audiences (who were watching a first cut minus the music score), which amounted to saying, "It was a good film, except for all the parts about drinking and alcoholism." That was, of course, pretty much the entire point of the movie.

But still, *The Lost Weekend* soldiered on and became their most significant critical success to date, going on to be nominated for seven Academy Awards, and winning for four, among them an Oscar for Wilder as Best Director and one for Brackett for Best Picture, and another which they shared for Best Screenplay. The film was placed on the Library of Congress's National Film Registry, which noted that "Director Billy Wilder's unflinchingly honest look at the effects of alcoholism may have had some of its impact blunted by time, but it remains a powerful and remarkably prescient film."

Ever restless and despondent over the corporate and public responses to *The Lost Weekend*, in between finishing the picture and its eventual release in the fall of 1945, Wilder would take on one of the stranger freelance jobs of his career, directing and editing *Death Mills (Die Todesmühlen)*, a documentary about the Nazi death camps made for the US government. During the Allied occupation of Germany, Brackett was at the studio talking with Wilder when Billy received the call from the discreetly named Office of War Information (OWI) offering him the chance to direct some propaganda material, a job that Brackett described as one "he can't and shouldn't turn down and which he is superbly fitted to fill. Feeling very widowed at the thought but gave my blessing."

This startlingly intense twenty-two-minute film, in German and English, could well have been subtitled "Proof." The film's concept, as commissioned by the government, was to educate the German people, and by extension the world, about the war crimes and genocidal atrocities committed by the Nazi regime. It was an abbreviated version of a much longer documentary work orchestrated by the British government that took many decades to fully complete. Its value was that it arrived much sooner on the doorstep of the world amazingly close to the conclusion of the war. The German-language version was first shown in the occupied US sector of West Germany in January 1946, with the rather prosaic title "German Concentration Camps Factual Survey."

It commences with a succinct indictment in a calm, cool narrative voice: "The following is a reminder that behind the curtain of Nazi pageants and parades was millions of men, women and children who were tortured to death in the greatest mass murder in human history." The actual images, drawn from footage of newly liberated concentration camps and presented accompanied by a stark modernist musical score, included shots of piles of corpses, naked skeletal survivors, as well as ordinary German citizens who were being forced to face the reality of what had occurred. Stuart Jeffries of *The Guardian* called it a "holocaust film too shocking to show" and observed, "Perhaps most moving of all are the piles of stolen personal belongings of gassed victims, filmed by the liberators of Auschwitz, as well as by US troops at Buchenwald. They included piles of clothes, shoes, toys, wedding rings, and gold teeth, destined for the vaults of the Reichsbank."

Sometimes it seems as if Billy Wilder was simply destined to make a government documentary about wartime atrocities, even though he must have thought that escaping to America as a refugee meant he might be fortunate enough to put all the madness behind him. His karma was both conflicted and convoluted, and yet also revealed a consistent continuity and an otherworldly skill at being in the right place at the right time. It had to have had an enticing but terrifying appeal when he was first approached by the savvy Elmer Davis, who had been a CBS radio commentator until he too was called upon to serve as the head of the OWI. And if he had not stepped forward to accept his government's challenge to document horror, he would probably never have returned to Germany at all, let alone consider using devastated Berlin as an on-location site for his next narrative film, after doing his duty.

Davis, himself an entertainment broadcaster whom fate had likewise led to contribute his communications skills to making history come alive, managed a huge official public relations and education branch of the government with some ten thousand skilled staffers around the world. Though familiar with Wilder from his position in the broadcasting industry, he first got an enticing glimpse into the man via *Life*'s profile of Brackett and Wilder in mid-December 1944 and saw something in Billy's background that might prove useful. And when he approached the émigré director with a request that he suspend his successful Hollywood career for a while to help the Allies "re-civilize" his homeland, little did he know that was about to change Wilder's life forever.

Wilder seemed, at first, an obvious choice for a patriotic project requiring both talent and tenacity mixed with personal affinity and compassion, but Davis did not realize how fragile the façade of Billy's personality really was. Terry Teachout touched upon Wilder's fragility in a piece in *Commentary*: "Gifted though he was at comedy, life was no laughing matter to Billy Wilder. . . . He saw up close the anti-Semitism that he described with typically caustic irony when speaking of the German people in old age, long after his mother and grandmother had vanished into the maw of the Holocaust: 'I know the decent ones, I know the indecent ones, I know the ones who stood outraged—but within them [all] there was a little jubilation: one Jew less. . . . I could have maybe have saved my mother—but I didn't dare, because then . . . there would have been one more.'"

That *has* to be one of the weirdest comments by a descendant of a generation of innocent victims ever made. Having fled Germany in 1934, when he saw the inevitable taking shape before his eyes, only to return nearly fifteen years later to witness the archival documentation of what he had feared so vividly, and view it for editing purposes, over and over and over again—that must have been beyond harrowing. I for one have absolutely no doubt that Wilder suffered from a mixture of post-traumatic stress conditions: one, a professional case of finding a way to illustrate an unreal reality, and two, a personal case of having left his mother and grandmother behind to perish in that reality. That existential guilt must have been an enormous burden. But what could have prompted him years later to make light of it in such a quizzical comment is beyond imagining, apart from being an expression of what psychologist Wilhelm Reich called "character armor," a survival device that surrounds a vulnerable identity structure with bombast.

The closest example I can think of in arts and letters is that of American author J. D. Salinger, whose experiences in the U.S. Army formed a similar crust around his character forever. Of course, in Salinger's case he was among the actual American soldiers liberating the camps and freeing the prisoners, at least those who were not encountered in mass graves, whereas Billy had to encounter the archival filmed evidence repeatedly so as to order it into some semblance of an educational film artifact. That closer proximity might explain how Salinger became Salinger, with his rigidly regimented Vedanta meditation practice being inexplicably mingled with his penchant for affairs with young writers such as Joyce Maynard. Whatever gets you through the night.

Billy Wilder never spoke about what he watched in acres of archival footage in order to reduce it to a twenty-two-minute instructional film. Instead, he simply let it seep into his consciousness, into the dim cellar where he stored the memory of leaving his mother and grandmother behind. And while in Berlin, a city he had compared to looking at the end of the world, he also began absorbing the ambient field of energy which would inform a new movie taking shape in his clearly tormented brain. As Sikov characterized his existential exposure so fittingly, "No building remained unscarred. The city was divided into four sectors, each ruled by the conquering army's military police. The people, living in squalor, were all but hopeless. For Billy Wilder, Berlin was the perfect location for a romantic comedy."

That amazing insight into the wayward mind and imagination of this creative but troubled man must also be coupled with the director's sheer power of raw will in convincing others of the veracity and necessity of his own plans, desires, or even whims. In the case of his sudden arrival at the crossroads of his next picture, amidst the personal trauma of loss and rubble, and the professional need to always be busy and productive, he was even able to explain to the U.S. Army the many almost plausible reasons for officially supporting him on his next entertainment venture by providing special privileged access to wartime sites in order to shoot a completely authentic love story right in the middle of the mayhem. Basically, Wilder wrote a dossier on what he called the "vital propaganda value of mass entertainment" and explained that a well-crafted human melodrama would have more impact than a hundred traditional newsreel subjects on the theme of liberation.

*   *   *

Billy would allow this notion to gestate while pursuing other helpfully distracting projects, among them coping with a personal upheaval only two weeks after going home to America: his wife Judith filing for divorce, citing extreme cruelty. He took that in his stride, just as he did everything else. One surprising event back in the States was the sudden upsurge in popular and critical interest in *The Lost Weekend*, a film he feared had been lost forever. After his expert tinkering had produced a fresh ending and he had added a new, unsettling musical score, his Paramount corporate handlers were willing to celebrate the commercial success of the film, and, naturally take credit for believing all along that it was a masterpiece. Seemingly overnight, it had become a success. Paramount was still careful enough, though, to open the film in London before America, with the *Hollywood Reporter* declaring that "London is on a praise binge for *Lost Weekend*. Even with the paper shortage it's gotten more comments than any picture since *Gone with the Wind*."

Meanwhile, perhaps to keep himself busy during Wilder's somber return to his homeland, Brackett had taken the open space of time as a bonus for himself, and produced a confection of his own, this time with his old semi-closeted director friend Mitchell Leisen at the directing helm. *To Each His Own* was released on March 12, 1946, and was based on an original story by Brackett about a middle-aged American woman named Jody Norris, played by Olivia de Havilland, who has a brief interlude with a certain Lord Desham (Roland Culver) during a particular night watch in London during the war.

Later on, her story of meeting a pilot, falling in love, and bearing his illegitimate child after he died in combat is told in flashback and memory. She tried to adopt her own child but was not allowed to, with the boy going instead to her best friend. The convoluted drama culminates in her son returning to London, himself now an American pilot, and pivots on the kindness of her old friend Lord Desham helping her regain a lost relationship with him.

Upon his return from Germany, and back in the saddle again with Brackett, Wilder paradoxically proceeded to make one of his even stranger companion pieces, shot during the summer of 1946. It was almost as if he was searching for an antidote to what he had just witnessed. Inexplicably, given his latest foray into the darkness of his own national and family nightmare, he decided to direct a supposedly jaunty Technicolor operetta set in fin-de-siècle Vienna called *The Emperor Waltz*, starring Bing Crosby. Conflicting private demons seemed to be urging him to move in all professional directions at once. Brackett was utterly clueless about the director's choice of Der Bingle, and apparently agreed to it merely on Wilder's recommendations, writing, "I don't suppose I ever understood it very well. I was sure Billy would know. After all, Vienna!" But Billy didn't, not by a long shot.

The less said about *The Emperor Waltz*, the better: keeping Crosby company during this almost surreal follow-up to *The Lost Weekend* and *Death Mills* were Joan Fontaine, Richard Haydn, Roland Culver, and Sig Ruman in a tortured romp about a brash American gramophone salesman in Austria at the turn of the twentieth century who tries to convince Emperor Franz Joseph to buy one single gramophone so the entertainment product might gain more favor with the Austrian public. (How, exactly, is never explained.) Since Crosby was Paramount's biggest star at the time and Wilder was the studio's top director, it was relatively easy to get company executives to greenlight a collaborative venture between the two. Wilder later readily admitted, in his usual fractured English, that "The picture didn't come out what I wanted. . . . I was looking back at my childhood in Austria—waltzes, Tyrolean hats, creampuffs—shutting out what came later on," a revealing reference to the obliterated cultural landscape he just finished visiting. "I would like to have done the picture as a tribute to Lubitsch. A tribute to Lubitsch, it was not."

To both the American Film Institute and *The Saturday Evening Post*, Wilder was typically candid on the subject of his hits and misses, giving the former his take on one of his most successful later solo films, *Irma la Douce*—"Yes, it was a huge hit. But I'm not sure why, it's a movie I don't think about too much."—and to the latter an explanation of how he dealt with flops like *The Emperor Waltz*: "We in Hollywood do not bury our dead. They continue to stink. They will stink next week in Cincinnati and in London, and two years from now they will stink on television. I have the capacity for erasing it from my mind." Alas, that capacity even extended so far as being able to erase partners from his mind when he no longer needed their cooperation. In fact, he started doing it almost at the inception of his and Brackett's amalgamation.

It's not like either of them had any chance to get their feet wet, or to learn the ropes in the industry that had already started feeding on their dreamtelling. They had been tossed into the deep end of the Hollywood talent pool right away, and the ropes were always tightly leashed around their necks—but in tandem, at least. The only certainty was that they were getting better and better and better at writing masterful screenplays; in fact, they were the best in the business. But concurrently, their temperaments were colliding at an equally impressive rate and making life a misery—a glittering and successful one, but still a misery nonetheless.

That musical operetta film with Bing was perhaps the partners' first genuine flop, or at least their worst creative decision, to date. Even the suits at Paramount detected the aromas wafting around the film, with no amount of Bing's singing capable of clearing the air, so they delayed its release for over a year. Thus, in the spring of 1947, Wilder took Brackett along with him back to Germany again, to set about writing a return to form, of sorts. It was to be a film shot entirely on location in the scarred city of Berlin, and has best been described as a "cynical comedy," but for me it's always been one of their most revealing accidental tragedies.

That film, *A Foreign Affair*, starring Marlene Dietrich and John Lund, would not see the light of day until 1948, a full three years after *The Lost Weekend*. The title's ironic pun on political affairs refers to a U.S. Army captain named John Pringle (played by Lund) in post–World War II Berlin, under Allied occupation, who is torn between two liaisons, one with an ex-Nazi club singer (Marlene Dietrich) and an overlapping one with the US congresswoman (Jean Arthur) who is investigating her. Its primarily serious tone rests on the ambiguity and ambivalence of the multiple and conflicting legacies of Berlin, and by extension, all of Germany. Arthur is perfect as the prissy and aptly named Phoebe Frost of Iowa who is looking in to rumors that the torch singer Erika von Schlutow was the mistress of either Herman Goering or Joseph Goebbels, or both, and that she is being protected by a never-identified American officer.

The congresswoman watches a newsreel of Adolf Hitler in the company of Erika and asks the Lund character—also from Iowa, but unbeknownst to her also Erika's lover—to bring her to headquarters so she can examine the singer's official personnel file. Weirdly enough, in order to distract the congresswoman, the captain proceeds to woo her. She is intensely proper but eventually surrenders to John Lund's incredibly bland charms. Meanwhile his colonel informs Lund that he knows of his affair with Erika but wants him to continue with it in the hope of being led to her more notorious former lovers. At the same time, Erika and Phoebe are arrested during a raid of the nightclub where Dietrich's character performs in a search for Germans without identification papers.

At the police station, Erika pretends to be Phoebe's cousin so she can secure her release without revealing her identity. Another of Erika's army of ex-lovers, a Gestapo agent named Hans Otto Birgel, is suspected of hiding in the Occupied Zone and jealously targets the Lund character before being killed by American soldiers, with Erika being arrested for her complicity. Phoebe and John are both reunited, in the climax of one of the most surreal films ever cooked up in the feverish brains of Brackett and Wilder.

One of the key distinguishing features of the film is its devastated and barren landscape, the defeated urban wasteland of Berlin itself, which is perhaps the true star of the movie after all. It was the same ravaged city Wilder had become fascinated by while serving as the documentarian for the US government. He had finangled a promise of official American support in exchange for making a movie about Allied-occupied Germany. It was an offer he couldn't refuse, allowing him to transmute some of his angst into what he imagined, with the help of Brackett and co-writer Richard Breen.

The producer Erich Pommer had been given the responsibility of rebuilding the once opulent and influential German film industry, and he was only too glad to cooperate in this mutually advantageous venture by giving the remains of the studio facilities and grounds at Universum-Film AG over to Brackett and Wilder. Among the many people Wilder interviewed in the assembly of his real-life raw material for the screenplay were people who were having great emotional difficulty with the disappearance of their once grand urban center. One of these was a woman who appeared to be clearing rubble from the streets, or at least trying to help. Wilder recalled later that the woman was grateful the Allies had come to fix the gas: "I thought it was so she actually could finally prepare a hot meal, but she said no, it was really so she could commit suicide."

In a piece of supreme irony and weirdness, *The Emperor Waltz*, their musical fantasy of Vienna would open on May 26, 1948, with their dour and bleakly gray saga of occupied and all but destroyed Berlin opening less than three months later, on August 20. What audiences were expected to make of the synchronicity of such overlapping, perhaps unconscious, dream and nightmare narratives was anyone's guess.

CHAPTER SEVEN

END OF THE LINE

Broken Dreams

"You're Norma Desmond, You used to be in silent pictures—you used to be big.

"I am big, it's the pictures that got small."

"Uh-huh, I knew there was something wrong with them."

WILLIAM HOLDEN TO GLORIA SWANSON,
SUNSET BOULEVARD

As if frozen in a holding pattern, Brackett and Wilder's partnership maintained its stasis but also its fruitful yield: there was always the next picture, and the next next one, each intersecting with the other in a way that brooked no withdrawal. I draw attention to the drastic scheduling overlaps between pictures written and produced because of the nearly vertiginous nonstop assembly-line techniques that rendered the partners almost unable to fully examine their situation. Obviously Brackett was writing about it constantly, but only whispering it to the privacy of his diaries, while Wilder was so busy being Billy, worrying about his health and welfare and planning his next triumph, that he barely acknowledged the existence of a calendar at all.

It had been in the first month of 1947, as the dramatic finish line of their amalgamated marathon was approaching, that the first mention was made of what Brackett called Billy's Berlin Story, *A Foreign Affair*. Incredibly, though, only one week earlier, on January 8, Brackett and Wilder were already talking about the germ of the movie that would be their final masterpiece together, after considerable mutation: "At the studio, Billy and I tried to evolve a new picture, discussed the idea for a comedy. It's funny but a little piddling. Mae West and José Ferrer were considered for the parts." They actually thought they might concoct a lighthearted comedy to soothe the wounds of their postwar piece, an antidote which of course would become darker, more sinister, and more sheer noir in tone than they could ever have imagined.

Somehow during this same period, Brackett, who had supernaturally found the energy to be the President of the Screen Writers Guild in 1938 and 1939, would once more summon the organizational mindset to soon become the President of the Academy of Motion Picture Arts and Sciences, an official role he played from 1949 to 1955. Perhaps that dual role of creative writer-producer, running parallel to his duties orchestrating the ongoing political and business affairs of a huge Hollywood professional membership association, gave him the wherewithal to sustain, survive, and soldier on with his irascible, volatile, mercurial, and occasionally downright nuts partner of more than the last decade.

While working on *A Foreign Affair*, and the skeleton of what would eventually morph into *Sunset Boulevard* at the same time, Wilder had commented, "You know, we will have more violent political disagreements on this picture than we have ever had." Brackett noted his private response in his diary: "Suddenly I thought, 'Oh no we won't, because I can't go through the disagreeableness of association with you any longer.'" Still the work continued, with Billy appearing to admonish Brackett: "This is the last picture we will do together. I want to do things more politically daring than you would permit. I want to stop working, to start when I want to. I am no longer afraid."

Brackett noted that he heard this with a mixture of consternation and relief, "for the stress of working on this picture has been hellish. We resumed writing." But for me the most remarkable revelation contained in Wilder's declaration was the inadvertent one: that he had formerly been afraid and thus had needed the guidance and tutelage of his elder mentor and writing associate. But now, his fear had abated, or else it had been replaced with towering arrogance. Either way, his newfound confidence, if indeed that's what it was rather than overcompensation or projection, seemed to hold him in good stead going forward, and would, clearly, result in him making some of his most successful movies, on his own. The slights just kept on coming, as when Brackett had attended a party at columnist Hedda Hopper's home for the owners of *Look* magazine, and the following day was told by Wilder, "Now you know why I don't want to work with you." Say what?

January 1948 had dawned with the customary mix of mayhem, mania, and movie magic, all agitated by the frenzied mood swings of Brackett's off-the-rails partner: "Billy is in one of his moods of revolt against Paramount and in the morning all for going to New York, but in the afternoon suggesting a contract with me to do four pictures in the next seven years." Unlikely, to say the least. It is always a challenge to keep up with the mercury of a manic-depressive, especially once you know that's what you're dealing with, and those are the cards you've been dealt. Brackett, ever the dedicated bridge player, decided to play his hand as best he could under the circumstances.

On June 7, Brackett's wife Elizabeth passed away, removing a source of both struggle but also a sanctuary from his convoluted life. He wrote, "I held my dear girl's hand, and very quietly, more quietly than drifting to sleep, the breathing stopped and I was left with a sharp sense of aloneness, of realization of how I'd depended on that wise, ill woman, how she'd meant home and refuge from the foolishness of this town."

He had been soldiering on during her protracted illness, and perhaps was intentionally distracting himself by producing another light, independent non-Billy movie, *Miss Tatlock's Millions*, about which Wilder curtly told him, "It's the worst picture you ever put your name on. Ever." It was one of those times that Billy was absolutely right. As if seeking the solace of the somewhat familiar, in short order Brackett would marry his late wife's sister.

As the end of July approached, the partners scrapped several ideas they had simmering on the back burner and decided to focus exclusively on the Hollywood story. Brackett described Wilder coming up with the "wildest, most arresting frame" for the movie: a body that, after being delivered to a morgue, begins telling his story to the other corpses there. It would become the opening scene in the first draft of *Sunset Boulevard*.

After being temporarily elated with his manic ideas, Wilder returned to his usual state mind the next day, which Brackett described as "Billy in one of his preposterous moods, a mood of resentment and suffering, brooding angrily most of the time, and all of the time a list of the faults of America. The only pleasure the country offers is to walk into Romanoff's and have everyone say, 'Look at that crazy man, he's beginning his picture with corpses talking at the morgue.'" In October, some of Wilder's depressed vibe seemed to be rubbing off on Brackett, if it hadn't already done so after a dozen harrowing years: "A dull lonely day at the studio . . . My worry is about the *Sunset Boulevard* picture, which I think lacks everything a picture concerning Hollywood shouldn't be: ugly, perverted, banal, in the producer-with-an ulcer way."

That ulcer continued to manifest itself through 1949, the final year of Brackett's diary entries, with almost all their energy now being devoted to their Hollywood story. On January 14, Brackett described his ongoing endurance dilemma in some detail. "I went to Billy's to work but Billy felt he was coming down with the flu and must have a penicillin-inhalation, and work, save for the briefest of ideas, was unthinkable." There was always, always *something* to interrupt their creative flow, whether Billy's alleged illness or Gloria Swanson's arrival. By February their prison sentence together was still achieving dismal proportions, as they tried to soldier on but had a "rather alarming day of trying to block out the remainder of the script and finding nothing but banal scenes and emptiness ahead." Further observations of Brackett often focused on the frequency of what he called "stalled and agonized days."

The year 1949 would finally end—feeling for Brackett as if there were several years of emotional and creative struggle packed into one single slot on the calendar—and with it, so did Brackett's journal of the secret life of Billy Wilder. "A quiet morning of conference with Walter Reisch at the studio. We played bridge until 11:30, tried setting the grandfather clock to the point of absolute accuracy, and all of us jumped into 1950." And the rest of us all jumped into the spooky dreamworld of *Sunset Boulevard*.

By 1950, a watershed year in the epoch of both their careers, Billy Wilder was ready to jump, too. To jump ship, and sail away as the captain of his own cinematic yacht, one with no partner to contain, restrain, or corral him. No one to require him to demonstrate a semblance of civility. Or, at least, not the same partner he had known since first arriving on America's dreamy shores.

Years after his arrival in America, Billy Wilder had quipped in his usual sardonic manner, "I came here because I didn't want to be in an oven." Going back must have been a huge challenge. I'm quite certain that Wilder had a nervous breakdown while visiting postwar Berlin to document hell, or maybe it was an emotional overload and meltdown. I'm not a psychiatrist or a psychologist, but it definitely seems that something had shaken loose inside of Wilder that continued to rattle around for his remaining years, leaving him sardonically bitter and coldhearted. Of course, the private comments, asides, and personal diary entries of his partner Charles Brackett quite often suggest that Billy was never exactly a fountain of human warmth to begin with.

Terry Teachout's piece in *Commentary* seems to concur with my only slightly over-the-top assessment of Wilder's state of mind and emotional health, although it stops short of actually asserting that he had a breakdown. (To be clear, my suggestion is not that he went nuts, so to speak, only that he shared a similar dissolution with F. Scott Fitzgerald, for instance, who wrote bravely about when the roaring Twenties stopped roaring in *The Crack-Up*.) As Teachout puts it, "Wilder spent several months in Europe viewing and editing death camp atrocity films. This experience, coming on the heels of the discovery that his mother and grandmother had almost certainly been murdered by the Nazis, solidified his barely disguised pessimism and disgust for the exigencies of human nature. And after two lesser efforts, he and Brackett made the bleakest and the most original of all their films."

Indeed, *Sunset Boulevard*, the 1950 film that would both make and break the team, was startling in its originality, overwhelming in its bleakness, and remarkably able to elicit drastically different responses from both viewers and industry members alike. It was also being made under a kind of internal and external duress that Wilder had probably been experiencing ever since fleeing his homeland in 1934 but had somehow managed to keep under wraps. The range of reactions would be as extreme as the style of the film. Hollywood mogul Louis B. Mayer approached Wilder after attending the official Paramount premiere screening and exclaimed, "You bastard!" He proceeded to berate and scream at him, shaking his face in Wilder's. "You have disgraced the industry that made you and fed you. You should be tarred and feathered and run out of Hollywood!" Billy, ever the succinct screenwriter, merely quipped a terse "Fuck you!" as Mayer stormed off into the crowd.

But quite a different reaction would come from the emotional actress Barbara Stanwyck at the same premiere. Most notably, she approached the star of the movie, Gloria Swanson, with tears streaming down her face. Stanwyck then knelt down, clasped her trembling fingers onto Swanson's ball gown, and kissed its hem, after which she rose and the two femme fatales embraced warmly in an expression of support that was apparently beyond words altogether.

What kind of movie generates such extreme passions on both sides of the appreciation or rejection scale? Well, a great one of course, but also a very complex one, too. A screenwriter, producer, and director don't really set out to consciously revolutionize cinema with one work, and certainly not to intentionally alienate an entire industry upon which they depend for their bread and butter. But if they are lucky, and if they are already hostages to their own fate, that can be exactly what happens. But given Wilder's duress, and Brackett's distress, it's still almost a miracle that the film was ever made at all.

Even after the obvious struggles that Billy's Germany stint had unleashed in him, and even though by this time being in the same room with him was an ongoing challenge for Brackett, they still found time to bestow their gifts on other directors for films that didn't even belong to them. Perhaps it was distracting and restorative, for instance, when they offered their services as script doctors on Robert Sherwood's screenplay for the 1947 Henry Koster film *The Bishop's Wife*, with Cary Grant and Loretta Young. Though they received no screen credit for this work—a common practice in Hollywood—one gets the definite feeling that whatever that snappy romantic comedy may have been before their ministrations, in all likelihood they gave the film much more of the taut beauty we associate with it today. They were simply that good.

By August, they were already at work on their new movie, which Wilder had taken to sarcastically referring to as "A Can of Beans," a false working title meant to distract and confuse the Paramount head office, but one which by all accounts Brackett took to be Billy's actual title. Brackett was feeling more and more out of place in their equation, with October finding him dealing with Paramount's offer of a new contract that seemed designed to "move him out to pasture." He started to feel as if they wanted him out of the way so they could more easily work out deals directly with Wilder. What's worse, as Wilder's writing partner and producer, even Brackett was not at all fond of the coldly cynical tone that Billy was insisting their new movie (eventually correctly identified for him as *Sunset Boulevard*) was going to have at its heart. Brackett even expressed his doubts to their loyal editor Doane Harrison, asking if there was anything they could do together to combat Wilder's "declared war with the American audience."

Brackett's diaries, though they don't contain specific references to his quarrels with Wilder on the film's subject and style, do convey that he was apparently still under the impression that they might continue working together through 1949, the year after hearing from publicist Herman Citron about the press release on their current projects and contracts—one that summarily announced that following this present film project together, Wilder would subsequently be a solo act. The worst part for Brackett was the fact that Billy didn't tell him personally, letting it come out publicly instead in such a perfunctory manner. Nonetheless, he wrote, "I gather that his near future will be dedicated to showing how much better his pictures will be than mine, and they may well be—but Paramount will be the loser, not I, and I'll be pretty busy making the best pictures I can make." The crucial thing to remember in all of this offscreen drama was that they still somehow needed to continue with the task at hand: writing, producing, and directing *Sunset Boulevard* together.

Their latest screenplay, the basic architecture for one of the greatest cinematic experiences since *Citizen Kane*, and one of the greatest films in history, was completed in a hushed first draft of sixty-one pages and submitted for scrutiny to their keepers at Paramount, with an unusual note attached to what they called the first act of *Sunset Boulevard*: "Due to the peculiar nature of this project, we ask all our co-workers to regard it as top secret." Incendiary in its content and overall attitude, it was a little odd for the screenwriters to refer to it as peculiar. What made it so, even in their minds? They seem to have known that it was lightning in a bottle which could at any moment blow up in their faces. For one thing, the original script treatment of this tale of corrosive celebrity, industrial-scale crassness, and descent into self-absorbed madness opened its narrative in a morgue with its narrator as one of the corpses.

Sam Staggs, a film historian whose study *Close-up on Sunset Boulevard: Billy Wilder, Norma Desmond, and the Dark Hollywood Dream* has the same quality of rapid-fire wit that this film celebrated, referred to it as "brutal boulevard," and with good reason designated it as "their mordant elegy to the silent-picture era, and by a decree of cross-eyed fate . . . the picture that ends the collaboration of Billy Wilder and Charles Brackett." Having already determined that their partnership was a strange kind of marriage, it is hardly surprising then that their divorce would be equally exotic. Everyone in the movie business knew this was going to be their last hurrah together, of course, since Billy had told everyone preemptively, but in a way, most movie lovers also knew it, at least those who picked up the fan magazines whose job it was to perform the same task carried out by the gossip cathedral of the internet today. Staggs is notable for his witty approach and florid film-lover attitude toward a classic film that has been called a poisoned love letter to the movies.

I'm also rather fond of Stagg's tongue-in-cheek delivery style, as it almost approximates the snappy dialogue of the filmmakers he was exploring during this painful waning of their illustrious careers. And he also realized that their pairing was almost marital in nature, sharing Sikov's sentiment that Wilder's "marriage with Brackett produced a lot of acrimony and eleven of the best, most successful films Paramount ever produced." They also saved the best for last, making of their farewell collaboration a film for the ages, one befitting the lofty ranks of film artists into which they had risen by dint of their own otherworldly skill and sheer stamina. As Staggs so clearly illustrated, in a strange way Wilder was also married to Norma Desmond, or at least to the Hollywood goddess myth she so corrosively embodied, and by telling her story, he hoped to tell the story of Hollywood itself.

When Cameron Crowe ask Wilder if his most famous film was a black comedy, Billy quickly and curtly responded, "No, it's just a picture." He didn't like being typecast. But nonetheless it was a black comedy, one of the finest, and yet it was also a film noir, one of the darkest, and by merging the light and the dark, it managed to create a true hybrid form that is best left outside of all classification. The film stars William Holden as Joe Gillis, a struggling screenwriter, and Gloria Swanson as Norma Desmond, a former silent-screen star who succeeds in enticing him slowly into her demented world, a world in which she imagines she will be making a triumphant return to the screen. Erich von Stroheim plays Max, her devoted and somewhat abused butler, and Nancy Olsen, Jack Webb, Lloyd Gough, and Fred Clark appear in supporting roles. Most notably, veteran director Cecil B. DeMille and gossip columnist Hedda Hopper play themselves, and the film also features exceptional cameos by several leading silent film stars, including Buster Keaton, H. B. Warner, and Anna Nilsson.

As I'm sitting in front of the first draft of their final screenplay, it strikes me that it's kind of the holy grail of blueprints for a masterpiece that would make them screen legends and pariahs at the same time. And, as is usual in the film business, it underwent significant transformations from their original idea to the finished visual elegy they crafted together. The morgue: let's begin our story, they somehow reasoned, where everything ends for everybody. The early version Brackett and Wilder toyed with was expected to launch us without hesitation into facing the real star of the movie: mortality.

In the original draft, Joe Gillis's corpse is wheeled into a room containing other bodies, under sheets and with toe tags. Once the attendant leaves, one body begins emitting a "curious glow," and then speaks in voice-over:

> *A MAN'S VOICE: Don't be scared. There's a lot of us here. It's all right.*
>
> *GILLIS: I'm not scared.*
>
> *MAN: How did you happen to die?*
>
> *GILLIS: What difference does it make? It'd make a good jigsaw puzzle, with the Hollywood columnists trying to fit the pieces together.*
>
> *. . .*
>
> *MAN: Were you an actor?*
>
> *GILLIS: No, a writer. I was having a tough time making a living.*
>
> *MAN: It's your dying I was asking about.*
>
> *GILLIS: Well, I drove down Sunset Boulevard one afternoon. That was my mistake.*

Their brilliant cinematographer John Seitz has also commented on the shift in focus the *Sunset* storyline took: "Originally we had it open in a morgue. God, we worked hard on that scene. But the head of Paramount thought it was too gruesome, showing bodies lying dead in a morgue with a dead narrator talking in the first person. There were all kinds of dead bodies around, including children. And then they were sort of resurrected in spirit, they were chatting with each other in the background. And it was chilling. They previewed it but then dropped it. It was a strange thing."

Dated March 21, 1949, the actual finished screenplay unfolds in a more conventional, although still unsettling manner, one less likely to have caused the corporate office powerbrokers to have simultaneous strokes:

> *Sequence "A": START the picture with the actual street sign: Sunset Boulevard, stenciled on a curbstone. In the gutter lie dead leaves, scraps of paper, burnt matches, and cigarette butts. It is early morning. NOW the camera leaves the sign and moves east, the gray asphalt of the street filling the screen. SUPERIMPOSED on all this are the CREDIT TITLES, in the stenciled style of the street sign. Over the scene we now hear sirens. Police squad cars hurtle toward the camera, turn off the road into a driveway with squealing brakes.*

> *MAN'S VOICE: Yes, this is Sunset Boulevard, Los Angeles, California. It's about five o'clock in the morning. That's the homicide squad, complete with detectives and newspaper men. You'll read all about it in the late editions, I'm sure. Because an old-time star is involved, one of the biggest. But before you hear it all distorted and blown out of proportion, maybe you'd like to hear the facts. If so, you've come to the right party. You see, the body of a young man was found floating in the pool of her mansion, with two shots in his back. Nobody important really. Just a movie writer.*

Still ominous in tone and disconcerting in its context, the film unspools its narrative about an almost deserted mansion on the famous street in question, where the police detectives examine the floating body of Gillis, while through flashbacks, the dead writer recounts his narrative. Six months before his demise, Joe is attempting to sell one of his story ideas to a studio executive—a Paramount executive, naturally. The writer overhears a script reader named

Betty (played by newcomer Nancy Olsen, who would become so disenchanted with the movie business that she abruptly changed her career plans) critiquing his story harshly, which gives him pause enough to entertain his already festering self-doubts. While trying to escape the repossession of his car, Gillis swerves into what he thinks is an abandoned mansion from the glory days of Hollywood. It is in fact still occupied by a former movie star named Norma Desmond.

Mistaken identity ensues when the spooky butler Max, played with consummate craziness by von Stroheim, ushers the writer into the inner sanctum, wrongly assuming that the writer is there to arrange for the funeral ceremony of the loony star's dead chimpanzee. Thrilled to learn that the undertaker is actually a screenwriter, Norma imposes on him to read and critique her own treatment for a new film she wants to make and star in, one about Salome. Although the script is woefully lacking in any merit, Gillis makes flattering noises, enough of them for him to be hired as her script doctor and collaborator. He surrenders to her demand that he move in to the mansion to work with her full-time on her obsessive project. Her butler has since explained that she is "emotionally fragile" and has already entertained suicidal urges, and also that *he* is the one who writes all the fan letters she so gleefully receives. Adding spice to this mix is the fact that von Stroheim was an actual director of one of Swanson's actual films from the silent era, 1929's *Queen Kelly*.

Gillis discovers to his horror that not only is he the sole dinner guest at her New Year's Eve party, but that playing along with the star's delusions—which includes her buying his suits and treating him as what he has become, her boy toy—has gone too far. When he tries to extricate himself from the worsening situation, he discovers that she has attempted suicide again, ostensibly because of his rebuffing her advances. He stays with her, fatefully, and continues working on an imaginary screenplay with young Betty at her office, while Norma proceeds to blindly insert herself into the studio executives' lives at Paramount. Eventually, Norma discovers that Gillis is actually in love with young Betty, that her butler is her only fan, that the studio only wants to rent her vintage car, that no comeback is in the offing for her at all, and that Gillis will soon be gone for good. He will be gone all right, but mostly because when he finally tries to disentangle himself from her tentacles and depart, she loses touch with reality altogether, murders him, and is led away by the authorities.

Although it is at the center of an unreal city devoted to dreaming with your eyes wide open, *Sunset Boulevard* itself is, of course, a real street with real houses, many of them residences of the real people who make the unreal dreams come true. It has been connected to the film industry since about 1911, the year the city's first film studio, the Nestor Film Company, opened there. The usual film workers lived modestly in the relatively normal neighborhood, up until the booming 1920s, when the level of money in the industry increased exponentially. Once the star system took root there, luxury homes, many renowned for their decadent glamour, began to take over the sprawling blocks, with many formerly big silent films stars still ensconced within the community. Wilder had always wondered what became of these figures now that the parade had passed them by, so to speak, and he began to imagine the story of a hugely popular silent film goddess who had lost both her celebrity and the box office appeal that always accompanied it.

The Norma Desmond character echoes several of these actual stars, with whom Billy would have been very familiar as an émigré ex-Berliner in the movie business who loved American culture and its films. Some echoes of the fading iconic motif can be located in Greta Garbo, Mary Pickford, Pola Negri, and Mae West. In addition, there were ample echoes of the mental disorders that so often went hand in hand with the celebrity of such stars, among them Mae Murray, Valeska Surratt, and the former It Girl, Clara Bow.

The museum curator and film critic Dave Kehr has also asserted that silent film great Norma Talmadge was the "obvious if unacknowledged source of Norma Desmond, the grotesque, predatory silent movie queen," in addition to observing the close parallels with Mabel Normand, a huge silent star who was murdered in 1922 in a still unsolved case. There was more than enough raw material to cull and work from in the drafting of their screenplay, but in mid-1948, perhaps aggravated by their personal animosities, Brackett and Wilder were frustrated with the slow results. They brought in D. M. Marshman, a writer for *Life*, to help them sort through their obstacles, merely on the basis of a positive review he had written about *The Emperor Waltz*, one of the worst films they ever made. No matter, since his true purpose may well have been to act as a buffer, a safety zone between the bickering writing/producing/directing line of fire that had become a trademark of the Brackett and Wilder franchise.

Even though they were still being very protective of their potentially incendiary story ideas and continued to conceal their full content from nervous front office censors and churlish studio executives alike (by only submitting one or two pages of writing per day, based on a nonexistent plotline), their keepers still demanded changes to satisfy the Hays Code, as enforced by Production Code Administration head Joseph Breen. An example of their hypersensitivity was the Breen office's judgment that some of Gillis's lines were too suggestive, requiring them to alter his off-the-cuff remark about his situation, "I'm up that creek and I need a job," to "I'm over a barrel. I need a job." Either way, only about one third of the script was even completed when filming started in mid-May 1949, and writers, producer, and director were unsure of how the story would actually climax.

One thing they did know was that it was a sterling piece of biting satire. And I'm in agreement with Julie Kirgo in her assessment in an entry for *Film Noir: An Encyclopedic Reference to the American Style*: "There are no belly laughs here, but there are certainly strangled giggles: at the pet chimp's midnight funeral, as Joe's discomfited acquiescence to the role of gigolo, at Norma's Mack Sennett–style entertainments for her uneasy lover, and at the ritualized solemnity of Norma's waxworks card parties, which feature such former luminaries as Buster Keaton as Norma's has-been cronies." I do believe that one of the most ideal characterizations for this utterly unique piece of film history is that of "strangled giggles," the perfect title for another film, all on its own.

As usual with the collaborative stranglers in question, accounts of the casting for the film vary drastically, with Brackett claiming that he and Wilder never considered anyone but Gloria Swanson to play the dotty Norma Desmond, and Wilder recalling that he at first wanted Mae West and Marlon Brando (perhaps when it was still a broad comedy), both of whom would have totally ruined the picture. Montgomery Clift would have been more suitable, given his own ambivalent identity, and he was intrigued by the story at first, before deciding to go off on a skiing vacation after finishing a picture, his third, with Olivia de Havilland called *The Heiress*. In addition, he may have been put off by the fact that in real life he actually was having an affair with an older woman, singer Libby Holman. Miss West was appalled at Wilder's invitation to play a nutty dowager, even though that's precisely what she herself actually was. Equally dismissive was the great, but seriously retired, Greta Garbo, with whom they had worked on their second Lubitsch feature, *Ninotchka*.

Wilder apparently also contacted the Polish silent star Pola Negri, but she was too Polish to be taken seriously for the role, and then Clara Bow, who was not interested in returning to movies acting as anything or anybody. Norma Shearer was also a logical choice to approach, but she disliked the script intensely, as did Mary Pickford, though they realized that requesting her to have an affair with a young man half her age was too non-Mary to even consider. According to Wilder, it was fellow director George Cukor who steered him in the direction of the regal Gloria Swanson, who, like the fictional Norma, had some difficulty making the transition to talking pictures in the thirties. In the end, Wilder felt that she would be the perfect match for an actor that Paramount already had under contract and could therefore simply be ordered to take on the task: William Holden, who admitted to being extremely nervous and doubting that he could pull of the portrayal. But he could, and he did.

While the relentlessly changing casting ordeal was taking place, it was mirrored by equally abrupt changes to the almost nonexistent screenplay, which at times seemed to have an organic life of its own that the partners needed to faithfully believe would turn out all right in the end, even if that end was a complete blank. By mid-February, Wilder, Brackett and their third wheel Marshman were still tinkering with the incomplete script. Marshman started to prove his true worth to the team when he provided alternatives to their either/or method of proceeding. For example, different accounts of whose original idea the story was invariably surfaced over the years, depending on who you were listening to. While both Brackett and Wilder agreed the film should be comedic, the question of how broadly the satire should be painted was always debatable, with Brackett seemingly opting for a funnier route and hoping to make an actual comedy about a silent screen star that he had been fantasizing about for years.

Neither of the partners, however, knew how to develop and embody this notion until they met Marshman, whose idea it was to have the senior silent star get involved romantically with a younger man. Wilder, in keeping with his usual instincts, wondered if they could have the older dame kill the young paramour. In general, Brackett wanted there to be a lighthearted tone, which was perpetually bumping into Wilder's appetite for darker, bleaker, sadder, and more sardonic angles and attitudes. Then again, an old friend of Wilder's, Armand Deutsch, also expressed his belief that the whole idea was Wilder's all along: "Billy once showed George Axelrod a scrap of paper which he had saved on which he had scribbled the words, 'Silent picture star commits murder. When they arrest her she sees the newsreel cameras and thinks she is back in the movies.'" Can't get more precise than that little story outline.

However their shared ideas materialized, though, as Sikov accurately noted, Brackett, Wilder, and Marshman "produced a script that twists comedy into something quite disturbing but never stops being bitterly funny, as long as one doesn't take their jokes personally." Which all of Hollywood did, inevitably. One can easily imagine the Greek satirist Aristophanes being deadly earnest when he lampooned the philosopher Socrates in Athens two thousand years ago, and just as easily imagine Socrates not being particularly amused himself. As Sikov notes, the script "contained lots of references to real people, each of whom had to agree to use their names. Some didn't. The starting date grew closer, and the usual tensions and egos of Hollywood filmmaking continued to surface."

* * *

It's often been noted that given their disparities and their chaotic working methods, it was an amazing achievement that Brackett and Wilder ever succeeded in creating anything at all, let alone something as historic as their shared masterpiece. What strange bedfellows these two writers were, any way you choose to look at it, and how mysteriously potent was the alchemy that resulted from their uneasy attempts to mix oil with water. That odd sorcery, which I've described as the strange magic of the game of double solitaire they played with each for over a dozen years, was a powerful but vulnerable kind of détente, one that grew to be the stuff of legend in their industry.

One of the keys to their longevity as partners was the simple fact that having so little in common, they rarely if ever socialized with one another. Wilder, correctly characterized as voluble, loud, obnoxious, cynical, and jaded, had enough of a challenge coping with his mild-mannered associate during their screamfests at the office, with Miss Hernandez waiting patiently outside in her alcove, waiting for the inevitable sheets of paper ripped out of Brackett's yellow legal pads for her to try to decipher, without having to endure him socially.

Billy liked parties, and he liked performing his chief role at them: himself. Brackett was not a partygoer, unless you count a quiet game of bridge with a few friends. For his wife Elizabeth, who before passing away had been a reclusive alcoholic anyway, going out much in public had never been a palatable option to begin with. His idea of a rousing good time, as *Life* described it, was to host weekend luncheons, described as "Hollywood's equivalent of Mme. de Staël's salons in 18th-century Paris. To them troop the most entertainingly articulate writers, actors, actresses, and assorted geniuses in the craft. Brackett, who is an appreciative listener as well as an excellent raconteur, presides over them with solicitude and grace. In this function he is ably assisted by his wife, a kindly but witty lady whose occasionally corrosive remarks have from time to time been attributed to Dorothy Parker." Everything is, eventually.

The novelist Christopher Isherwood, one of the many literati who was seduced into going to Hollywood, confided to his diary a slightly different account: "Sunday luncheon we went to the Bracketts—why, God knows. Yesterday had a really funeral party at the Bracketts. Perhaps the most boring people I've ever known." And according to Wilder biographer Maurice Zolotow, guests could be seen at their modestly modern stone house on a Sunday, "ladies and gentlemen sitting in Belter chairs around Belter card tables playing cribbage with an antique cribbage board." More than a few observers familiar with the Bracketts' milieu have pondered if Charlie and Billy alluded to, whether consciously or unintentionally, these overly sedate parties in the staging of the infamous card game scenes at Norma Desmond's mansion, with multiple near-cadaverous ex-stars shuffling their cards ominously.

But if one solution to disliking each other so much was never to hang out together, another aspect of their working method has also struck historians as well. They may have been among Hollywood's greatest writers, producers, and directors, but they were also, according to the surmise of Staggs, "a pair of cutups and loafers . . . [who] couldn't get a grip on their story of a forgotten silent film star in a ramshackle palazzo. Successful collaboration demands two or more strong personalities who recognize their strengths and acknowledge their weaknesses." That was something the pair did amazingly well in the beginning and middle stages of their movie romp. In fact, when he was once asked for a Screen Actors Guild contract to define the meaning of a "team," Brackett arch response was, "Whom God hath joined together."

"Writers with implacable egos," concluded Staggs in his study of *Sunset Boulevard*, "should work alone. Certainly, neither Wilder nor Brackett was deprived of ego. As movie veterans, however, they accepted the total collaboration required in filmmaking at every step." Together, they shone, up to a point. And to witness this shining, even from a distance, was to be beguiled by something inexplicable: a typical day of work consisting of certain essential ingredients, with the fights being at the top of the list. But also, the noisy kibitzing from Billy and more playful shenanigans from Charlie, constantly seeking ways and means to work together, as well as procrastinate.

A. C. Lyles, a Paramount producer prone to wandering around the stables of his champion cinematic racehorses, noted Wilder constantly puffing on cigarettes or cigars and whacking furniture, while Brackett "conveys an impression of sound metabolism and repose, which his friend finds soothing." I enjoy the Staggs distillation of the equation: "Static body, vigorous mind, these Brackett attributes balance Wilder's fitful nerves." Lyles also took in the tenor of their working space, roughly the size of a hotel suite with an office, a smaller room for playing cribbage or cards, and a large bedroom into which they might both retire for a nap after lunch, after entertaining visitors. They "wrote when they felt like it."

Wilder's take on their arrangement was classically fateful and almost existential in its dark tones: "One of the great things about a collaborator is that he stops you from committing suicide. It's fun to arrive in the morning and have forty-five minutes of bitching about your wife, and how you saw a picture and it stank. It establishes a good atmosphere before you get going on your own crap. Writing is a very dull and boring, dreary thing." Wilder was also quite conscious of the results if the two were not together in the same confined cell: "At the end of the day, he has seven pages, and I have nothing, because I read a pornographic novel, wrote letters, or slept."

Brackett, meanwhile, perhaps because of his own very conservative and serious senator's-son upbringing, was guilty of having an opposing work ethic, if Billy could be seen as having one at all. Five years after their split, Brackett recalled how their mysterious method of working actually worked: "It began with talk—seemingly endless talk—but all of it directed towards the project. The only reliable peg I know on which to hang a story is character." Wilder claims the two had caught brief flashes of Norma Desmond five years before they got around to shutting themselves in together in their office to go on a blind date with the addled star.

"What sort of story shall we do?" Brackett had enquired, to which Wilder pondered but had no reply, until some of the hubbub in the outer offices seemed to suggest a tantalizing theme, "a relationship between a silent-day queen and a young man." In Wilder's account, they came to bring in D. M. Marshman because he "was bright, and we thought we might go stale so we brought in somebody." Even though both Brackett and Wilder knew the ins and outs of building drama as well as anyone in the business, since their only real obstacle was each other, once Marshman entered the field (he has been described as the catalyst that changed the dynamic from a dysfunctional love affair into an exciting and liberating threesome) the truly juicy plot developments starting coming fast and loose.

Brackett and Wilder, along with their new buffer Marshman, clearly liked to live life on the edge. Preproduction shots began on March 26, 1949, and continued through April, with the screenplay still unfinished when the official shooting schedule began on April 18. In communicating with their longtime cinematographer, John Seitz, Wilder was able to use his customary shorthand technique combining elements of farce and implication, as when he dictated, "Johnny—keep it all out of focus—I want to win the foreign picture award." During a sensitive scene of Norma Desmond lying in her bed with her wrists cut open, when Seitz asked for some direction, Billy quipped, "Johnny, it's the usual slashed-wrist shot," and for the monkey's funeral scene, Seitz was "directed" with "Johnny, it's the usual dead chimpanzee set-up."

This strategic approach only works of course, when you're dealing with two things: a genius as your cameraman and an old collaborator who already intuitively understands what it is you want, so they avoided shooting on brilliantly sunny LA days, in favor of rare foggy or gray-toned skies that suited the mood more effectively. Two aspects of film noir were consistently recurring motifs: the first-person narrator's voice and the optical presence of *Stimmung*—an atmosphere that Robert Porfirio, paraphrasing Lotte Eisner, has described as "an aura. It's most often diffused with a veiled, melancholy landscape or an interior in which you have the glow of a hanging lamp, or even a sunbeam shining through the window"—with both being used to great effect in *Sunset Boulevard*. Wilder liked to demystify most working methods as much as he could, and in an interview later in life he addressed the voice-over, a device he helped to make almost ubiquitous among his peers: "I have always been a great man for narration, and not because it is a lazy man's crutch. That might be true, but it's not easy to have good narration done well. What I had in *Sunset Boulevard* for instance, the noir narrator being a dead man, was economical storytelling. The mistake is in telling you something in narration that you already see, but if it brings a new perspective, then it's good."

Personally, from my perspective the customary use of a voice-over narrator in noir is worth noting as a modern evolution of the ancient Greek tradition of a chorus on stage that provided context and commentary about the tragedy unfolding in the actors' performances. The chorus shared privileged insights and intimately reflected details in exactly the same manner as the usually sedately toned narrator's voice floating over so many noir dramas. If there is a voice-over to be used effectively in noir scenarios, that voice needs to be as distinctively monotoned aurally as the light is optically.

The use of light as another kind of voice, a visual narrator, so to speak, to tell a story, is also something masterfully crafted in *Sunset Boulevard*, a film made up almost exclusively of interiors. It's hard to believe now, but originally the team had planned to make this film in color before deciding that dark monotones would be more suitable, not because it was noir, but because it was right.

The neo-noir director Paul Schrader has given us insight into the actuality of noir versus its assumptions: "Film noir is not a genre. It's not defined by setting and conflict but rather by the more subtle qualities of tone and mood. It is a film 'noir,' as opposed to the possible variants of film gray or film off-white." Likewise, Wilder further explained his relationship with light, also the result of working with John Seitz, as follows: "You can have all kinds of *stimmung*. You can have very gay, romantic *stimmung*, any film by David Lean has a lot of *stimmung*. Then there's the idea that there's a certain kind of

California house where I would sense that as the sunshine comes through, that it has not been dusted, the dust is floating around, and I tried to get that kind of *stimmung* into Gloria Swanson's house in *Sunset Boulevard.*"

However, no matter how carefully devised and worked out the visual mood was, the domain of John Seitz was still of course always at the mercy of the writing and scheduling panics of the director, and when Seitz responded to a compliment about his photography for *Sunset* being very somber and low-key, his response was revealing: "Well, that was appropriate to the mood of the story. Again, Billy often never had a finished script. On *Sunset Boulevard* for instance, we didn't have a finished script until just before the picture was finished shooting." Asked whether Billy actually did not know the ending or whether he just did not write it down, Seitz responded even more revealingly: "No, he just guessed at it, he and Charlie Brackett."

They had to have been two of the luckiest artisans working in movies, or perhaps the most talented, or maybe a magical mixture of both. In addition, their consistent flair for aligning themselves with the best talents in the business to make their own talents shine all the more, well, that ability to creatively collaborate with other gifted craftsmen might have been one of their most significant and inherent gifts. Besides, they desperately needed to take frequent breaks from each other in order to survive at all.

Like most exceedingly clever creative strategists, Brackett and Wilder were always capable of surrounding themselves with the best of the best, and then, mostly, just letting them do what they did. This was never more true than in the case of the film's photographic visionary. I totally concur with Wilder's contention that John Seitz should have won an Oscar for his cinematography on *Sunset Boulevard*, crystallizing and distilling the dramatic effects he had developed for both *Double Indemnity* and *The Lost Weekend.* The film's spooky, shadowy black-and-white photography was the result of

Wilder trusting Seitz's style and judgment to allow him to make his own decisions on how to capture the story visually.

Film historian Tom Stempel has stated that "In both *Double Indemnity* and *Sunset Boulevard*, Seitz does something which has always impressed me. Both are films noir, and he finesses the fact that both are set in the sunniest of locales. . . . He brings together the light and dark in the same film without any seams showing." And neither were there any seams in the remarkable art direction of Hans Dreier and John Meehan, whose task it was to create the "unforgettable decaying grandeur" of Norma Desmond's deluxe dream house of horrors, which Seitz would then photograph with such a decisive and evocative vision.

One element about which Wilder was adamant with Seitz: the corpse of Holden's Gillis character *must* be seen from the *bottom* of the swimming pool, a special effect that was challenging but worthwhile. The camera was inserted inside a specially designed box and lowered underwater, with multiple experiments failing to satisfy Wilder. The staggeringly powerful shot was finally achieved by actually placing a mirror on the bottom of the pool and filming Holden's reflection from above, with the distorted images of the onlooking police officers forming a very surreal backdrop to the inaction. Seitz to the rescue, as per usual.

Wilder was, as usual, unrestrained in his description of his desired camerawork: "You will not find in my pictures any phony camera moves or fancy set-ups to prove that I am a moving picture director. I like to believe that movement can be achieved eloquently, elegantly, economically, and logically. Without hanging the camera from a chandelier and without the camera dolly dancing a polka." True, shooting downward at a mirror to make it appear to be looking upward was not by any means a "phony camera move." It was sheer Seitz genius. That technique was almost parallel to the sophistication in their screenplay together, which the website Cinephilia and

Beyond characterized as "One of the most haunting, memorable, and honest depictions of Hollywood ever created. . . . The greatness and importance of *Sunset Boulevard* lie not only in its technical mastery, in Brackett and Wilder's dark but humorous script with several of the most frequently quoted lines of all time, or even in the career-defining performances of these great actors. A good deal of the film's value stems from its audacity: it took a lot of talent and expert maneuvering to get the film made with regard to the Production Code."

When *The Paris Review* interviewed Wilder about the source of his ideas, he was typically laconic and downplayed his obvious gifts, claiming that he didn't know where his ideas came from. He just "got them"—sometimes even at the toilet, where he kept a little black book to make entries containing scraps of dialogue he had overheard. But the idea for *Sunset Boulevard*? "For a long time I wanted to do a comedy about Hollywood. . . . The picture industry was only fifty or sixty years old, so some of the original people were still around. Because old Hollywood was dead, these people weren't exactly busy."

Such was Billy's ability to manufacture dreams, not only the ones that we all adored watching in theaters, but also his living memories, even the dreams inside his own head. As chronicled in Brackett's private diaries, their impending split, in the shadow of which the two men were spinning the web of what would be the finest film of either their careers, appears to have been somewhat liberating, both in some good and some not-so-good ways. According to Matthew Dessem, "Their fights got worse; ashtrays and telephone books were thrown."

Wilder's nasty and cynical wit, blended almost seamlessly with what Dessem calls Brackett's "doomed romanticism and sense that an older way of life was under assault by modernity," managed to merge in some profound manner. Teachout's account in *Commentary* captured both the intensely brilliant weirdness of their final film as well as some of the animus that fueled its slow but steady forward momentum: "All but operatic in its quasi-Gothic expressive intensity, it is also noteworthy for the genuine sympathy with which its characters are portrayed, as well as the nimble verbal wit that leavens a loaf that could easily have become too sour for general consumption."

Luckily for us, their shared work together always stopped mere inches from that borderline, allowing them to soldier on in the fractured fabrication of a film that Wilder would always designate as "revolutionary for its day." One thing is certain: it was Wilder who wearied of working with, writing with, or simply sharing the spotlight with his longtime creative partner. Equally obvious was the fact that no matter how tough and occasional brutal *Sunset Boulevard* felt, it always maintained a crucial humanizing balance provided by Brackett's opposing temperament, without which it would have slid headlong into the morass of Billy's unbridled desires, since he just as clearly wanted to make his future films utterly saturated by an even harsher tonal sentiment, even the superbly funny ones. But that balance came at a cost: the loss of Billy's good manners, however slim they may have been, and the stroke that took Brackett away in slow motion. The brilliance of the balance beam they seemed to personify for so long, however, never arrived without pretty much perpetual daily struggles.

Then came a series of what seemed an interminable number of retakes, reshooting certain scenes to make them more agreeable to the film's meticulous taskmasters, including the morgue scene, the pool scene, and some of Norma's more wild closing scenes. Seeking perfection has always been expensive, of course, and their film was suddenly almost a quarter of a million dollars over budget, though the corporate office was still confident about the picture's artistic value. The suits—having since learned the true content of the story, and that it was about Hollywood, not about a can of beans—did agree with the writer/producer/director team that the subject and theme would greatly benefit from being initially screened outside of Los Angeles proper.

Once the jagged and tingling musical score by Franz Waxman was added, something deep and even more disturbing seemed to click into place. Film music historian Christopher Palmer noted that the nerve-racking score contained the entire vibe of the film in miniature, with its ambient notes "trilled, jabbed, and pecked out, heavily accented, syncopated . . . beneath the racket of roaring, screeching brass and motoric rhythms . . . reflecting ingrained hopelessness."

They had apparently pulled off a cinematic coup, and nearing its release, trade papers such as *Variety*, *Motion Picture Herald*, and the *Hollywood Reporter* all generally applauded it, despite how disturbing they admitted they found its subject and theme. The latter paper extolled its virtues quite enthusiastically: "That this completely original work is so marvelous, satisfying, dramatically perfect, and technically brilliant is no haphazard Hollywood miracle but the inevitable consequence of the collaboration of Charles Brackett and Billy Wilder. You want to applaud *Sunset Boulevard* frame by frame."

The world premiere took place in August at Radio City Music Hall in New York. The film had become an unlikely success, with Paramount even anticipating a raft of awards to come—and many did come, although not the Best Picture Oscar that Wilder so coveted. (That one went to another Hollywood exposé that year, Joseph Mankiewicz's masterful *All About Eve*.) It was nominated for eleven Academy Awards and walked away with three, including Best Story and Screenplay for the partners, Best Art Direction for Hans Dreier, and Best Scoring of a Dramatic or Comedy Picture for Franz Waxman. They were however just as favorably lauded by the Golden Globe Awards, winning Best Picture, Best Actress for Swanson, Best Director for Wilder, and Best Original Score for Waxman.

Theirs was not, of course, the first film to try and take a scalpel to the bloated bodies of Hollywood's dream factory. That trend had started practically at the very inception of the industry. Rudy Behlmer and Tony Thomas outlined an early fascination with what went on off-camera in their history, *Hollywood's Hollywood* and located the allure in Vitagraph's 1908 production *Making Motion Pictures*, which was kind of an early documentary made when such pictures were then under a decade old. Silent cinema was already fascinated with itself and basked in its newfound glory in Mack Sennett's *Mabel's Dramatic Career* (1913), Charlie Chaplin's *His New Job* (1915), Cecil B. DeMille's early exercise in self-aggrandizement *We Can't Have Everything* (1918), and a movie from Lasky Studios (prior to morphing into Paramount) called *Hollywood*, which memorialized the dream that anybody, almost, could succeed there if they wanted to hard enough. Such self-reflection, although usually of a flattering sort, continued apace into the era of sound pictures, with *What Price Hollywood?* (1932), *The Death Kiss* (1933), the aptly named *Hollywood Boulevard* (1936), and, perhaps most famously, *A Star is Born* (1937).

But those films used their scalpels with restraint. And none before *Sunset Boulevard* had undertaken to execute an autopsy on the still-living body which housed the industry they were probing in a style that almost amounts to cinematic vivisection. As usual, the Staggs tone of voice is among the most compelling in this regard: "*Sunset Boulevard* is . . . as black as obsidian, and as lustrous. . . . Watching it is a painful pleasure because our illusions are mangled along with every character." Wilder's fellow director and admirer, George Cukor, had a rare and insightful take on *Sunset Boulevard* when he noted, "There's a lot of humor in *Sunset Boulevard*, but it's very important that the characters never feel they're being funny. It has to be subtle to be great fun, which it was, on both counts."

The great auteur critic Andrew Sarris, who found himself having to reappraise Wilder's output with more appreciation after first panning his early efforts, even the good ones, captured some of the ironic stance of Billy's personal and professional style in an insightful way: "Of Wilder, I can say what I once said of Lubitsch, that his films bridge the abyss between humor and horror. I would venture the hypothesis that every film that Wilder writes and directs represents an attempt to express the complexity of his feelings which have evolved over years of eager exile. The great dramatic moments in so many of his films could not have emerged if he had not had the courage to be profoundly honest with himself."

The nineteenth-century English speculative novelist Samuel Butler, author of *The Way of All Flesh*, presciently concurred: "Every man's work, whether it be literature or anything else, is always a portrait of himself, and the more he tries to conceal himself, the more clearly will his character appear in spite of himself." In this regard, Zolotow's characterization of Wilder is the most accurate one I've ever encountered, and I totally agree that far from what he defensively presented to the world, he was indeed a disappointed romantic at heart: "Young man, driven out of Europe by evil, a masquerade of cynicism and sarcastic wit, but under the domino the tender look of a romantic, whose heart was broken."

One feature on the film website Not Coming to a Theater Near You shared the general surprise of those outside the industry to news of the real story behind Brackett and Wilder's myth of inseparable creativity: "Since their separation, it has come to light that the 'happiest couple in Hollywood' was as much a fiction as any of the many masquerades that frequently appear in their scenarios. Though their polar opposite personalities blended so perfectly on the screen and on the page, in real life things were not always as harmonious." Wilder's assessment was somewhat diplomatic in this regard: "The success of *Sunset Boulevard* may have been part of our problem. Where do you go from there? I had some ideas he didn't like, and he had some I didn't like. The sparks just weren't flying anymore."

In the end, the last working project together laid bare some of their own skeletons on both a personal and professional level, and in the same way that Cinephilia and Beyond characterized that final film as a sobering exposure of the dark side of Hollywood, it was an equally sobering exposure of the dark sides of Brackett and Wilder. Brackett's diaries in particular reveal a bewilderment with his formerly close partner's strategic moves. He confided to a friend, "I never knew what had happened, never understood it." He found Wilder's apparent gratuitous cruelty "a blow, such an unexpected blow, I thought I'd never recover from it. And in fact, I don't think I ever have."

CHAPTER EIGHT

AFTERMATH

All Things Considered

The question about a picture is not whether it's good or bad, but whether it's alive or dead.

BILLY WILDER, 1950

In August 1950, as *Sunset Boulevard* was being released, Wilder was interviewed by Philip Scheuer for the *Los Angeles Times*. It was clear that one of his new mandates, in addition to reinventing himself from the ground up, was also reinventing the story of his ascent. Thus began the building of his own personal Wilder mythology, the one in which his genius was so innate that he never really needed anyone's support or creative scaffolding. He conveniently left out the part about needing to learn the English language from scratch, and availing himself of the former drama critic of *The New Yorker* in order to accomplish this little prerequisite.

In fact, when he sat down to talk with Scheuer for his suggestively titled profile titled "Wilder Seeks Films with Bite," he was in a far-ranging and expansive mood with an appetite for clarifying everything that had come before that very moment. How exactly he might surpass the "bite" contained in the two Oscar-winning noir classics he made with Brackett, he never did quite specify. He told Scheuer, "Class in pictures nowadays has to be smuggled in like contraband, and artistry is a dirty word. But if movie-goers would just talk about the last one they've seen for fifteen minutes, it would be very gratifying. That's all we in Hollywood ask." To which Scheuer cannily observed that "Wilder, who is likely to have his wish now that *Sunset Boulevard* . . . is in general circulation, thinks of himself as a writer who is lucky enough to be able to follow through on his own yarns."

Chief among those yarns may have been the myth that he was solely responsible for every inch of his success, a story that would gain momentum and scale with each passing year of his independence. But of course, that lucky writer also had two new collaborators and a new associate producer to assist him in doing everything by himself: Lesser Samuels and Walter Newman to write with, as well as eventually the great I. A. L. Diamond, and William Schorr to associate-produce. In Wilder's account, "All I try to do is get myself a story, splash it on the screen, and get it over with. And I try, for God's sake, to have news in every picture I make. To open up, to unroll a problem is interesting enough. We don't have to know the answer too!" He makes it sound almost easy. It never was and it never would be. Scheuer quoted Wilder as saying he and Brackett parted ways "because the studio wanted to get two pictures a year out of us instead of one. So we split up. He gets another director and I get other writers to work with, but I sure miss him." Oh, the joys of hindsight. "I always make things very tough for myself, by not going out and buying a successful stage play or novel but starting, instead, from scratch. The wonder is that *Sunset Boulevard* every got made, for that reason alone: usually a studio prefers to bank on a sure-fire property."

For the future, Scheuer echoed Wilder's chief belief that audiences want "anything with bite" and that "humor is a risky commodity these days." Perhaps so, but *Sunset Boulevard* did in fact get made, with both sharp satirical bite and dark humor aplenty, and one of the chief reasons was the longtime collaborator Wilder had just dispensed with.

Richard Gehman commented that Wilder's successful attempt to take Hollywood by storm was fraught with challenges from the beginning, chief among them learning English, which he did mostly from the radio and the American girls he enjoyed wooing. Up until his lucky break came, he was paired with Brackett and was able to almost communicate. As Gehman put it in a 1960 *Playboy* profile, "Wilder and Brackett became legends. . . . They were known for the ability to work anywhere—in barber chairs, while playing cribbage, or at parties. . . . Then they made *Sunset Boulevard*, one of their best. In 1950, at the peak of their partnership, they split up. . . . Neither will say exactly why."

Both have said exactly why, many times, although those reasons vary depending on who tells the story. Partly, it comes down to the remark made by a character in the great Nicholas Ray's film noir classic released the same year as *Sunset Boulevard*, one also focusing on a tormented screenwriter. Ray's *In a Lonely Place* contains the holy-grail line which explains how to survive working with someone you basically can't stand being with: "the chance to achieve immortality," which for a screenwriter and director means making a masterpiece that also makes money and garners awards, is worth *any* sacrifice you have to make to achieve it. Almost.

In the case of the formerly happiest couple in Hollywood, both the partners had to make sacrifices, of course; it's just that one had to make more of them, more often. Whether Wilder ever actually realized how difficult he was to work with, to even be with, is debatable. Manic depressives are not that well known for their startling insights of self-discovery, but he did recognize the Yiddish concept of *beshert*, something inevitable or preordained, as being active in the apparently random decision to pair him with Brackett. "I thought it was a fine idea," he told Burt Prelutsky for *Michigan Quarterly*

Review much later in his life, admitting, "I already had great respect for Brackett. He was much older than I was and had written several novels and many fine pieces for *The Saturday Evening Post*. I had no confidence when I was first starting out because I only knew English from going to the movies. After Brackett and I split up, I found it too lonely to write by myself. I find I miss having a collaborator, a sounding-board, someone whose taste and ideas I respect. Also, having a collaborator makes you come in to work on time."

For Matthew Dessem, the creative divorce appeared to be a necessity, at least from Wilder's perspective: "He did what he had to do, to move forward. . . . But even if Wilder had all of Brackett's finely taught courtesies, nothing could have masked the fact that they were no longer equals. It's unforgiveable to cause pain for art's sake. But in this case, the pain was a given. Brackett and Wilder's final days of writing together show that both men understood art's power to transmute that pain into something immortal." There it is again, the immortality incentive that was always being dangled in front of creative artists, especially those toiling in the dream factory of Hollywood, one of the few places on earth that such immortality might even be a possibility, if the necessary sacrifices are made.

For Sam Staggs, who has specialized in examining the entire architectural design of *Sunset Boulevard* and has deeply considered how or why no other structure could ever be designed by that same team, Billy Wilder's outsider status was key: "His syntax in conversation and interviews is not the syntax of a Wilder picture—not *Sunset Boulevard*, not any other one. Rather, the language in a Wilder film, and its flow, belong mainly to Brackett, to Diamond, or to any other collaborator in Wilder's career. The wit, the verve, and probably much of the plot no doubt come routinely out of Wilder's mouth. If there were a perfume called *Sunset Boulevard*, it could be said to waft through Charles Brackett's novels," citing especially *American Colony* and *Entirely Surrounded*.

Jim Moore also had some salient personal insights into their highly charged equation, and commented that his grandfather Charlie Brackett was not quite as staid as many imagined him to be: "Billy Wilder brought a certain irreverence that sometimes rankled my grandfather, I think, but nowadays people who write about him or Billy say that [he] was too genteel to do the things that Billy got involved in." Staggs reminds us that this is a limited view, one which might change if more people read Brackett's novels, which he characterizes as urbane, edgy stories, impatient with bourgeois values, dark, and even cynical. "Perhaps Brackett, despite his avuncular looks and his Republican milieu, saw the world as not such a genteel place, meaning that not all the darkness came from Wilder. In his writing, however, Brackett trimmed the fat from his vision to avoid excess, just as Wilder, in his best pictures, controlled his own directorial bad taste and cynicism."

In the end, I totally concur with Staggs that the only valuable way to prove much at all about the Brackett-Wilder partnership is through a close viewing and careful analysis of their films: "That's the evidence that counts—the rich result of their twelve years together. And those pictures are skyscrapers. By contrast . . . the ones Wilder made post-Brackett conform to standard studio building code: they're bungalows, storefronts, cabins, warehouses . . . and toward the end, the property is condemned."

And while he never actually denied its importance outright, Wilder did tend to downplay the contributions of his early creative collaborator, usually in his signature off-the-cuff manner. So it was all the more poignant, not to mention startling, when in the fall of 1949, after their masterpiece was finished but prior to its official premiere, Brackett met with Wilder in their office.

Before any work could commence, in Brackett's account, "Billy smiled that sweet smile of his at me and said, 'You know, Charlie, after this, I don't think we should work together anymore. I think it would be better for both of us if we just split up.'" Brackett was left without a single appropriate word in response.

Then, a couple of months after the public release of *Sunset Boulevard*, on October 20, 1950, Louella Parsons announced via the *Los Angeles Examiner* that Charles Brackett had resigned from Paramount Studios. He went sideways, to Twentieth Century Fox Studios, under Darryl Zanuck, where he remained active as a writer and producer for about twelve years.

That shift too signaled a sea change in the world of Wilder, whose volatility was already well known. According to Zolotow, even before *Sunset Boulevard*, he had undergone a distinctive transformation: "In his own eyes he had always been a genius. Now his opinion had been confirmed. . . . But now, his ego swollen beyond even the customary Hollywood megalomania, he strode the make-believe streets of Paramount like a conqueror. He trampled roughshod on the sensibilities of any and all persons on his periphery."

Up until that point, Brackett had chosen to endure the *Sturm und Drang* that emerged with the making of their postwar Berlin movie, mostly because Wilder had apparently pledged to him that their next film would be a tenderly touching story about a faded and possibly nutty silent film star who decides to make a comeback. What could go wrong there? It was supposed to be, in his hopeful mind, something of a high-minded comedy, and Brackett still harbored a personal fondness for the light comedy-of-manners mode. This tale, he was reassured, would reverse the customary storyline of a young hopeful actress coming to Hollywood to pursue her dreams and focus on a once legendary star who was suddenly living in her own imagination, outside the ranks of those who dream at all and left only with an amusing cacophony of comedic encounters. Supposedly, in the end she would triumph over all those who had forgotten her.

But Wilder, whose postwar European sensibility had come to embrace a high degree of unalloyed cynicism and pessimism, had shifted the emphasis, slowly at first and then rapidly, to a more dour and depressing state of almost complete reality collapse. This slow-motion cave-in of the famous actress's self-image was accompanied by a lot of the attitudes and behaviors that might envelop a loopy narcissist, and it was many of these elements that disturbed and eventually angered Brackett. Some of them, such as the sequence of Swanson as Desmond submitting to a rigorous regime of beauty treatments to restore her luster, he found offensively vulgar. William Schorr had become Brackett's associate producer for this project and he recalled a screening of early scene rushes when the two partners actually came to blows over scenes that Brackett, as producer, wanted cut, and Wilder, as director, wanted left in.

Schorr sided with Wilder and Brackett stormed out of the screening room. That was the point at which Brackett may have washed his hands, at least psychologically, of attempting to navigate the precarious partnership any longer. It was almost certainly the point at which, as Wilder confided to Schorr, it became clear this would likely be the last film he would ever direct with Brackett, allowing Billy to stride unobstructed into indulging some of his more lurid impulses. Among the many such urges would be his compulsion with opening and closing the film with scenes of dead people in morgues talking to each other about their fate. Even though that particular conceit did not survive the final editing process, it was an ideal metaphor for the kind of mayhem that can ensue when an artist has enough genius to know they're gifted, but not enough humanity to realize the important power of limits. As many have observed about this film, it walks a fine line between farce and tragedy, just as their entire partnership had done, and in many ways it erases that borderline altogether.

The rubicon had finally been reached. As Matthew Dessem notes, on March 29, 1951, Brackett and Wilder, along with D. M. Marshman, accepted the Academy Award for Best Story and Screenplay, with Wilder approaching the stage from the side opposite the other two. It should be further noted that just as they had entered that ceremony from separate ends of the stage, as if further memorializing their memorable partnership with an apt final metaphor, so too did they leave the stage in different directions.

Going off in different directions, that might well be, but going back where they came from? No, not literally, not to Saratoga Springs for Brackett, nor to a vanquished and vanished village in Austria for Wilder, but rather each one returning to their native emotional domains, each under the command of their own distinctive stylistic imprimaturs. Back to their own unalloyed natures, even: one a light-hearted and genteel affect, and the other that of a rough-and-tumble street urchin. It might thus appear that their own natural habitats would never intersect or collide again, except for the fact that they both stayed in the same jaded business, each performing the same functions, in the same insular city of tempered dreams, just as they had been before.

They could now each be fully themselves exclusively, each without the bother of interacting with their opposite's shadow, and without its interference in their work, which both thrived and suffered as a result. Brackett would retain his composure as a scion of social privilege and man of letters, turning out reliably entertaining diversions. Wilder would retain his nervous edge as an outsider with survivor's guilt, turning out consistently controversial social satires. Both would be acclaimed, from different directions, by the bestowing of Academy Awards from the cinema establishment. Brackett was forever insulated by his blue-blood exterior; Wilder was forever haunted by his exiled émigré escape from hell.

Joseph McBride spends considerable time in his Billy chronicle establishing just how profound and pervasive Wilder's displacement and ongoing survival mechanisms contoured basically all of his work, whether comedic or tragic: "The Holocaust shadowed Wilder's life and work in America. His failure to do enough to get his mother and other relatives out of Europe in time, or to ever see them again after 1935, tore at him in ways seldom discussed. . . . Wilder may have tried long and hard to cauterize the emotions he felt about the Holocaust, but he could never bury them." His delicate psychic condition was also explored in both "The Double Vision of Exile," an essay by Nancy Steffen-Fluhr, who analyzed the camouflaged Holocaust themes that were concealed in many corners of his overall work, and also by Gerd Gemünden in his study *A Foreign Affair: Billy Wilder's American Films*, which sheds light on Wilder's strategies for getting double and even triple meanings past the somewhat paranoid Hollywood censors.

Wilder's "suppressed rage" over his precarious condition as a Jew in Berlin was accentuated, like so many of his innocent countrymen, by his inability to do anything effective in retaliation, and this is the core of McBride's most useful insight about Billy becoming Billy: "Issues of lack of empowerment, frustration, and self-defensiveness, both physical and emotional, would find haunting echoes in many of Wilder's films. However disguised their origins and diverse their expression, these are pervasive obsessions underlying what is often simplistically described as the 'cynical' surface of his work. . . . I often feel that those who consider Wilder cynical fundamentally misunderstand his work."

Brackett and Wilder were both utterly devoted to the 80 percent of any film that is written dialogue, to be privileged over those other visual aspects, considering a screenplay to merely situate the physical space where the actors speak *their* lines, while being photographed doing so. And they both pursued their own respective upcoming independent film ventures with the sense of a nearly religious reverence for words in general, and *their* words in particular.

Truth be told, that actually meant they would each be fueling the weaker portion of themselves, in one case making self-indulgently cruel movies (while missing the necessary presence of a dike wall reading *only this far and no further*), in the other case making soft-centered confections that distracted audiences from reality (while missing the inspiring presence of a talent which knew no limitations on self-expression at all, saying *take a chance, life is short*). Brackett, meanwhile, would more easily wear his romantic projections of American values on his sleeve, making later post-Billy films that echoed a rather basic Republican attitude toward the mythology of America, one which tended to buttress or prop up some of the scaffolding of a rapidly fading American dream.

*   *   *

Keeping in mind McBride's admonitions to not misinterpret or over-interpret one of Wilder's key character traits, or even personality quirks, that of a hardened cynic, I recently decided to re-view, literally view again, certain prominent cynical Billy-esque celebrations of life's dark side, but looking at the films—*Double Indemnity*, *The Lost Weekend*, *Sunset Boulevard*, *Ace in the Hole*, and *The Apartment*—from a different vantage point. I tried McBride's perspective: maybe it was truer to consider Wilder a disappointed and disillusioned romantic, and a very sad one, rather than the more customary, and far too facile, interpretation of him as a cold-blooded nihilist cynic. And as with those tragedies, so it was with a revisit to *Ninotchka*, *Midnight*, the scintillating *Ball of Fire*, and the surreal *The Major and The Minor*.

The results of this experiment were most worthwhile: they revealed an entirely different film underneath my first viewing. Not just another layer of meaning, but a totally different movie altogether, one with a surprisingly different emotional temperature, that of the classical morality tale. Most of the equilibrium in Wilder's work had been provided by what Andrew Sarris has described as Brackett's "restraining, civilizing influence." The main characters in that little constellation of films, and all those they interact with, take on quite a different aspect, almost an existential vibe, if you will, when we presume that Wilder is a brokenhearted empath, rather than what he's more customarily imagined or presumed to be. Wilder, and Brackett too, for that matter, are both more like melancholic masquerade participants, playing a part in their own daily lives, than mere objective observers absolved of all feelings. The fact that they bring this melancholy tone to the surface via movies so sensitive and insightful is due in large part to the shimmering genius of their mutual author's voice.

By a strange coincidence, unless it was synchronicity, my watching *Ace in the Hole* took place just after completing the section of our tumultuous story having to do with their final noir masterpiece together, when I happened upon a TCM broadcast of the later film: Billy Wilder's first solo effort after "divorcing" Brackett. I had seen the 1951 film several times previously, of course, but it seldom resonated in quite the same way as it did while watching it from a retrospective point of view. So I sat back with a glass of wine and my notebook, prepared to venture once again into Billy's post-Brackett domain. My instinctive initial response was even more severe than my first viewings had been. It was one of the most depressing films I've ever seen. In fact, I could barely scribble any observations about it. But also, I must reluctantly admit, it was one of the most visionary.

In the end I found it necessary to watch *Ace in the Hole* spread out across a whole week of intermittent visits to the toxic and claustrophobic world it depicts. It's a world we now all appear to occupy together, in reality, over seventy years later, and it's no less toxic and claustrophobic when it has been translated into our digital society and transmitted globally via social media and the nebulous realm known as the internet. In fact, no surprise, it's far worse to have had circumstances transpire that have transformed this nasty media tale from the feverish imaginings of a gifted but problematic person into the everyday life that stares us in the face via Facebook, Twitter, and

Instagram, to name only a few of the many ways and means we have of alienating each other in real time.

In his interview with the *Los Angeles Times'* Philip Scheuer, Wilder remarked that "We are a nation of hecklers, the most hard-boiled, undisciplined people in the world." That seemingly negative characterization is all the more startling when one realizes that he was actually commenting with *pride* on the national character of his adopted homeland. He was also touting the state of mind, or of the heart, of the perceived audience for his new sensational film featuring Kirk Douglas in the most unflattering role of his career, as well as the viewers he imagined for the even more biting movies he planned to make in the near future, once all those past impediments, such as decorum or good taste, perhaps, had been removed from his personal and professional trajectory. The film is virtually marinated in meanness and venom. In some ways it seems not only to be a film about an utterly cynical solipsist, but also a film written and directed by one, too—maybe even one for whom the close examination of occasional human flaws was a subtle form of character camouflage for his own.

For me, one stunning realization is the fact that since *Sunset Boulevard* came out in August 1950 and *Ace in the Hole* followed it so rapidly in June 1951, it seems obvious that Wilder must have been working on both projects simultaneously. To some degree, both films are morality tales, and both examine, from different angles, the power of celebrity and fame as it stealthily operates in our daily lives. The disgraced reporter, played so vividly and aggressively by Douglas, who will stop at nothing to attempt to resurrect his journalistic career by capturing the attention of the press for what he initially casts as a human-interest story, is a poisonous cipher for the entire contemporary audience.

Accurately characterized as a biting examination of the often questionable and too intimate relationship between the media, the news items it reports, and the techniques used to report on them, this film also demonstrates in a prescient manner just how easily a gullible public can on occasion be controlled and manipulated by those charged with informing it. The reporter Chuck Tatum, brought to venal life by Douglas, finds it impossible to do the right thing to help Leo Minosa, a man who has innocently been searching for artifacts and becomes trapped in a collapsed cliff dwelling. The most logical form of rescue would be for engineers to shore up the existing passages and retrieve Leo, which would take about twelve hours. But Tatum convinces the local sheriff and contractors to take the much longer approach of drilling from the top of the mountain downward.

That decision, made partly to help the sheriff in his reelection campaign, stretches out the so-called rescue to a full week instead of one day, during which the reporter continues to saturate the front pages of national papers in his vain quest to regain his former glory. In the meantime, the public has been whipped into a frenzy of combined schadenfreude and lurid soap opera, gathering in ever growing numbers of cars, trailers, tents, and visitors (who are being charged admission to this tawdry circus atmosphere), all of which has an impact on the livelihood of the entire town.

Tatum, who has been wounded in an altercation with the trapped man's wife, slowly comes to his senses when he realizes that the drilling method has prolonged his story but shortened Leo's life. He remorsefully tries to confess to murdering the trapped man in order to help his exclusive story grow in scope and scale, but his editor cuts him off and fires him before he can write a new and more truthful account about what has happened during the week since the cave-in.

Responses to the film's bleak, misanthropic, antisocial undertones were loud and vociferous in their condemnation, with Bosley Crowther of the *New York Times* calling it a masterful film, but chastising Wilder, who "has let his imagination so fully take command of his yarn that it presents not only a distortion of journalistic practice but something of a dramatic grotesque, badly weakened by a poorly constructed plot, which depends for its strength upon assumptions that are not only naïve but absurd." The *Hollywood Reporter* declared it "Ruthless and cynical . . . a distorted study of corruption and mob psychology that is nothing more than a brazen, uncalled-for slap in the face of two respected and frequently effective American institutions—democratic government and the free press."

My main observation in this regard is that it is probably true that such was the case in 1951, but what of the brave new world of right-wing extremist news journalism of today? Is it not right at home in the polluted industry exemplified by social media and propaganda "news" networks for whom profit and viewership has replaced authenticity and accuracy in reporting? In our current world of fake-news purveyors accusing everyone else of being fake news, is this sad and seedy tale not just another day at the office? I'd hazard a guess and say that this dark, twisted fable was downright prophetic.

And yet despite the critical and popular rancor, the film still garnered for Wilder an Academy Award nomination for Best Story and Screenplay, and a Golden Lion at the Venice Film Festival, which also bestowed its prestigious International Award for Best Director on him. In 2007, the often astute Roger Ebert went out on a limb and stated that "Although the film is fifty-six years old, I found while watching it again that it still has all its power. It hasn't aged because Wilder and his co-writers . . . were so lean and mean. The dialogue delivers perfectly timed punches. . . . There is nothing dated about Douglas's performance. It's as right-now as a sharpened knife." Of course it is, because we all now live in its sordid world every day. And in a kind of redemption of sorts, in 2017 the National Film Registry of the Library of Congress selected it for inclusion. Its shadows continue to lengthen and its gritty message continues to resonate with our reality in shocking ways.

Ace in the Hole is also a movie with a series of firsts for Wilder, who by this time was beginning to regularly be referred to as an auteur: the first time he was commanding a picture's creation as the writer, producer, *and* director; the first film he made subsequent to his breakup with longtime collaborator Brackett; and also, unexpectedly, the first time a Wilder film was both a critical and a commercial failure. It's too easy to simply say that the film was ahead of its time, though that is true. There was more to the public and industry's rejection of his first solo venture than merely being dazzled by a genius who sees the future. They were also experiencing considerable nausea, of the existential variety, at their exposure to something so dark, so menacing, and so unremittingly venal.

Many have observed that once he climbed to the top of the award-winning Hollywood mountain, Wilder planned to stay there completely on his own terms, without any partners to stand in his way, as he shifted his focus from the merely noir aesthetic of *Sunset Boulevard* to one of utterly bleak and total blackness being unveiled via *Ace in the Hole*. All of the film industry, and most of the more avid cinema buffs, were well aware that Wilder had availed himself of the skills of varied screenwriting teams, and that now he was on his own. It was clear that he always needed to have another writer in the office with him, whether or not he accepted their input. It was equally well-known that, for whatever reason, he was practically unable to write alone, by himself, in solitude, without a sounding board against which to bounce ideas back and forth.

One such writer, Walter Newman, an inexperienced twenty-year-old radio scribe whose play Wilder had listened to on his car radio one night, was called to Paramount and invited to co-write *Ace in the Hole* with Wilder and Lesser Samuels, an ex-newspaperman and studio contract writer. With somewhat lesser mortals at his beck and call, the newly minted auteur was able to make short shrift of the composition process, one that featured a coldhearted examination of human beings on their worse possible behavior. Clearly, Wilder was giving full rein to his inherent misanthropic tendencies as he explored the outer edges of self-serving media drones as well as the average American, whom he portrayed as an enthusiastic sap capable of turning a tragic event into a circus-like bonanza of heartless entertainment.

Shot pretty much entirely on location in New Mexico, the film almost has the accidental feeling of a documentary as it relentlessly traces the steps by which a trapped man is monstrously used as a prop in the inflation and sustaining of a news story. It still shocks us even today, and must have completely blown the minds of moviegoers and critics alike back in 1951, when it arrived like a festering wound on the unprepared screens of America. One viewer described having felt like they had been beaten up by the movie. This was the project by which Wilder came to be known as such a cynical artist, and he was denounced for a gratuitous assault on the newspaper and television industries at the same time.

Wilder, stung by the almost universal disdain and displeasure at his first solo effort, was adamantly Billy and dug in his heels even deeper: "Fuck them all—it is the best picture I ever made." But the damage had been done, though even he shouldn't have been surprised at the reaction, which is often what happens when all limitations imposed by the cooperation of other professionals are removed and only the solitary ego of the auteur matters. Wilder even had a new secretary at Paramount, Rosella Stewart, an innocent who replaced Helen Hernandez when she decided to move with the more even-tempered Brackett after he left Paramount for Twentieth Century Fox. Unlike Hernandez, Stewart would have been unaware, apart from his reputation, of Wilder's quirks, foibles, weaknesses, or strengths, and she would have been much less likely to cast questioning glances at his barking.

Paramount itself, however, being well aware of his history, both the good and bad parts, was much more forthcoming in its brusque judgments about the direction in which Wilder was heading. He began to imagine people looking the other way when he entered the studio cafeteria, and started counting the former friends who were less enamored of his new footloose and independent persona. His studio bosses were not enchanted by the consensus of critical assessment that there had never been an American film quite like this one before. That much was very true, and in true capitalist fashion, they responded in the usual way, which strained their relationship yet further.

Wilder had a contract with them that stipulated that he had the right to determine the final cut and the movie's title, but "Without my consent and without even consulting me, [Paramount studio head] Y. Frank Freeman, having decided *Ace in the Hole* was a bad title, changed it to *The Big Carnival.*" Naturally enough, in this case at least, the director's title was the far better one. Wilder never forgot this slight, or the corporate reaction to his craftsmanship: "That picture, *Ace in the Hole*, lost me power at the studio." His spleen continued to rule his character, to the extent that people interacting with him began to realize that there was more than one Wilder. As Zolotow assessed his character armor: "There is coarseness in his films, as there is in his nature. . . . But when he talks to the press it is only cynicism he displays. Is this the real Billy Wilder? Yes. Is it the only Billy Wilder? No. There are many 'real' Billy Wilders."

One of his early and chief biographers, Zolotow searched in vain for what he referred to as the source of Wilder's ruling passions, "some crucial event, some series of occurrences, perhaps, which had been so traumatic in nature that they had engendered this powerful thrust of his imagination. I could not find it." That author has shared an encounter with Wilder's daughter Victoria, who intimated her own need to comprehend her father's challenging character: "I hope you will explain him to me in your book. I love him but I don't understand him. Never did. Wonder what made him the way that he is?" Join the club.

Two additional biographers of Wilder have wondered the same thing, in divergent ways that I think come close to the target of comprehending his complexities. I applaud their work, only slightly because it tends to concur with my own conjectures, and find that *Some Like It Wilder*, by Gene Phillips, and *Dancing on the Edge*, by Joseph McBride, each add a certain clarity to the Billy conundrum. Both McBride and Phillips have made the case that Wilder was not so much a hardened cold cynic as a drastically disappointed romantic, and this fresh angle of inspection helps to explain many of the man's obscurities. McBride also astutely draws our attention to issues relating to the Jewish identity in Hollywood, and indeed America at large, in a way that emphasizes my contention that Wilder suffered from a distinctive kind of survivor's guilt, on top of his post-traumatic stress.

Even though *Time Out* called *Ace in the Hole* a "diatribe against all that is worst in human nature with moments of pure vitriol," and *TV Guide* called it "a searing example of Billy Wilder at his most brilliantly misanthropic," and Slate opined that "if film noir illustrates the crack-up of the American dream, then *Ace in the Hole* is an exemplar of the form," all three press outlets still agreed to designate it a movie that stands as one of the great American films of the 1950s. Wilder himself eventually got quite used to referring to *Ace in the Hole* as "the runt of my litter," although the sting of the overwhelmingly negative critiques had to have disappointed him greatly.

The critical assessment of Wilder's profoundly disturbing first solo venture, and of his work in general, was fleshed out very publicly in print at the time of the controversy surrounding his first post-Brackett movie. The prestigious film journal *Hollywood Quarterly*, later to evolve into *Film Quarterly*, published a fascinating pro and con attack and defense of Wilder's first solo film, and by extension his entire ethos, in their fall 1952 issue, when the controversy was still hot. It was then further stoked by a rather unusual editorial decision for that highly respected supplement. The *Quarterly* may have bitten off more than it could chew when it commissioned Herbert Luft, a film editor and research/production affiliate in addition to being a screenwriter and producer of television films, to create a profile of Billy Wilder.

Since it was the year following *Ace in the Hole*, the editors might naturally have anticipated some degree of negative judgment, but what they received—a frontal assault on not just his newest film, but all his work—must have taken them aback. They felt compelled to balance their coverage by ironically seeking out a counterpoint to Luft's position, especially since several of the films he lambasted also fell under the auspices of Wilder's former writing partner and producer, Charles Brackett. Hence, this preamble to what ended up being a two-part essay on Wilder, called "Two Views of a Director," featuring Luft's piece, "A Matter of Decadence," and Brackett's, "A Matter of Humor."

Brackett's piece was preceded by a note from the editors, who wrote that they "recognize, in printing Mr. Luft's article about Billy Wilder, that the author's viewpoint is not an entirely objective one but has been formed by his bitter personal experience. For this reason they asked Mr. Wilder's friend and one-time collaborator, Mr. Charles Brackett, for the comment which follows. The two pieces certainly do not say the last word about Mr. Wilder's work, but they point up one distinction he shares with few of his contemporaries— he is one of the rare directors of this cautious day whose work may be called controversial." It was, of course, ironic, to say the least, since Brackett and Wilder were no longer friends (a fact that the editors must have known well), but they knew they could count on Brackett, as a professional, to put aside any of his personal animosities and address the issue of his former partner's role as an artist and entertainer.

Luft begins by extolling the virtues of Wilder's early and quite revolutionary work on Robert Siodmak's groundbreaking cinema verité piece, the quasi-documentary *People on Sunday*—which was produced by Moritz Seeler, and which a twenty-three-year-old Wilder conceived—calling it "the first time the camera looked upon real people" and one that is "still regarded as one of the finest examples of screen art." But things go downhill from there, and fast, as Luft charts Billy's manic course from the bottom to the top of Hollywood's heights (and to a much higher position than he himself had ever achieved, one might add). "Wilder's career is one of the most fascinating success stories in the cinema. With the rise of Nazism, the young writer goes to Paris where he becomes a full-fledged film director (*Mauvaise Graine*). Thus, with an actual directing credit to his name he arrives at the Hollywood scene in 1935."

As Wilder himself had commented, "I dragged my carcass up and down Hollywood Boulevard and starved for around a year and a half before I sold two original stories." Thus, Luft is off to the races in his description of Wilder's somewhat giddy rise to fame and glory, chronicling his initial collaboration with Brackett on the screenplay for *Bluebeard's Eighth Wife*, through films such as *Ninotchka*, *Hold Back the Dawn*, *The Major and the Minor*, and *Five Graves to Cairo*. He notes that "it was not until 1944 that Wilder, with *Double Indemnity*, established himself as a truly unorthodox film maker."

So far so good, one might observe. But then Luft makes an abrupt right turn, emphasizing that after his initial prewar films, something changed Wilder's trend: "Though he had watched the pulse of Hollywood and had learned the mechanics of motion picture making, seemingly without regret he turned from the media of his much-hailed Academy Award winner (*The Lost Weekend*) to more and more controversial subjects such as *A Foreign Affair* and *Sunset Boulevard*. Twenty-two years have passed since Wilder, having discovered the common man on the streets of Berlin, comes forward with another reportage, an item about a fellow newspaperman (which could have had an affinity with his own life). *Ace in the Hole* unravels the tragedy of an unscrupulous reporter who has skidded to the bottom of the ladder into complete moral and physical disintegration. Here Wilder has conceived an asset of characters who appear totally repulsive and whose reactions are never normal."

Luft acknowledges that Wilder makes news in every picture (perhaps that being his chief complaint) but also asserts that, paradoxically, he uses the same method of ruthless exploitation that he portrays negatively so often on the screen, "oversimplifying complex human emotions in order to bring out his utterly cynical viewpoint." In *Double Indemnity*, the "later Wilder deals with the aftermath of war with the luxurious cynicism of a sophisticate who has acclimatized himself to the ivory tower of Beverly Hills."

Luft proceeds to consolidate his critical position by admitting that there are many viewers, and readers, who might scold him, saying we shouldn't take movies so seriously, but such people are forgetting that films have becomes the universal language of our era, and that, as such, these days the screen is accepted as a veritable image of life itself. "There is," he writes, "a distinct pattern in the work of Billy Wilder that leads us to conclude that he is undoubtedly amused by the callousness of our time. *Sunset Boulevard* sets another bad example for this country. It presents a distorted Hollywood setting wherein it unravels the tragedy of a love-hungry actress who refuses to admit that she has grown old. Wilder's 'Hollywood' is ice-cold, calculated theatre, far from the American way of thinking and out of step with the real ideals of the film industry."

Now of course, Luft was not alone in finding the atmospheres conjured up via the sad spectacles in *Sunset Boulevard* to be oppressive and overwhelming. The great Pauline Kael shared some trepidation as well: "The whole enterprise exudes decadence like a stale, exotic perfume. Yes, you might not want to smell it every day, but then in

1950 you didn't get the chance: though it was certainly a change from oceans of rosewater, lilies of the valley, and that scrubbed, healthy look." But unlike Luft, she was still capable of appreciating the virtues, uniqueness, and exoticism of a magnificent work of malevolent art.

Luft then proceeds to focus on what he believes to be the decadent atmosphere of Wilder's world, calling him a master of systemically developed sensationalism, topping everything off with his own bombastic finishing touches. He judges that, all in all, "Billy Wilder's later pictures are of a shockingly deteriorating nature. His heroes have no integrity and expect none from anyone else. To him, Americans are a frightening array of ruthless, perverse, and criminal elements." Given his personal experience in the concentration camps, Luft is of course totally entitled to contrast his views with those of the director. "The America of Billy Wilder is not the America I found when I came to this country after living in Nazi Germany for six years. For me, as for the vast majority of newcomers, America has meant a symbol of freedom, not a hoax. Somewhere, somehow, like so many other Hollywoodians, Wilder seems to have lost his human heart on the way to the top."

But what if, given the most recent social and political developments in American society, Luft's America actually turned out to be, if not a hoax, then certainly a carefully crafted mythology, one that a capably creative and insightful artist such as the brazen and garish Wilder somehow saw through much sooner than anybody else? What if the corrosion of the American dream, its myths and self-inflated exceptionalism, has always needed the corrective measure of caustic eyes such as his? What if his heart had always been in the right place, but his disillusionment and disappointment were so deeply felt that it had become his mandate to expose something rotting at the core of that myth?

Which is why the responsive article by Charles Brackett is so informative as an alternative to the usual Wilderesque perspectives.

Brackett was still able to see the art behind the seeming coarseness and the method of his madness—although he, too, absolutely loathed *Ace in the Hole* upon first viewing. Brackett told Garson Kanin about the almost universally reviled first solo Wilder project that "Billy used to say he thought that it failed because it was too tough. I don't think he's right about that. Tough is all right. I admire toughness. I don't admire hardness. That picture wasn't tough. It was hard. But then, Billy's hard, isn't he?"

Yet Brackett still also knew fine craft when he saw it, in addition to recognizing something that Luft, and so many other people, had overlooked completely: the muffled laughter behind Wilder's savage satire. Hence his take on Luft's clumsy mishandling of his former partner's entire oeuvre, which is all the more impressive when one realizes that Brackett was still at the time in the middle of his tenure as President of the Academy of Motion Picture Arts and Sciences, ostensibly a corporate symbol of the very sacred cow that his former partner was so fond of roasting.

"I read Mr. Herbert Luft's article about Billy Wilder with a certain amusement. It's like reading an essay about Van Gogh by someone who is color-blind. No—more than that—this appraiser of Van Gogh is made actively ill by the painter's favorite color. Mr. Luft not only doesn't like a joke, he detests a joke. This is a limitation of nature to which one should be charitable. Certainly Mr. Luft's tragic experience in a concentration camp should cause one to overlook it. But in choosing Mr. Wilder for his subject, Mr. Luft has thrust his deficiency on the reader in a way that cannot be ignored."

Brackett goes on to describe Wilder's sense of humor as "the outstanding trait of the young man with whom I started to work some seventeen years ago. He was sassy and brash and often unwise, but he had a fine, salutary laugh. . . . Let us observe the conduct of Mr. Luft when he happens on a joke. He shudders first, then begins to weigh it on sociological and ethical scales—and alas, those scales aren't working very well."

Brackett also takes issue with Wilder's supposed animosity to America: "The indifference-to-America thesis runs into some difficulty when our essayist reviews *Arise My Love* and *Hold Back the Dawn. Arise* was a comedy with serious undertones and was decried by every America-firster as warmongering and jingoistic. In it there are tender and adoring references to America—and I can testify that they were put there by Billy Wilder. . . . *Hold Back the Dawn* was certainly also a bouquet laid at the feet of America by two people who loved it dearly."

In the end, Brackett even includes a qualified defense of *Ace in the Hole*: "It told the story of a ruthless heel. No one was asked to like or admire him. The story of him using the victim of an accident to rebuild his shattered career was not a pretty one, nor was it presented as what any newspaperman would do under the circumstances, but it did point up certain cynical qualities of the press and certain appalling habits of behavior in crowds who gather to watch events charged with misery. It was in the vein of American self-criticism which has been a major current in our national literature since the days of *The Octopus, The Pit,* and *The Jungle.* Because he was born in Austria, is Billy Wilder to be excluded from that vigorous and important trend? I don't think so."

CHAPTER NINE

ITERATIONS

Coasting Home

Never ask a big man for a small favor.

CHARLES BRACKETT, FIVE GRAVES TO CAIRO

I've always found it rather touching in the extreme how Brackett rose up to defend his ex-partner from what he perceived as unfair or ill-considered critiques, despite having been ditched so unceremoniously at the end of their mutual careers, and after being on the receiving end of perpetual bitchiness during their shared projects. But Brackett was, first and foremost, an industry professional and insider, and secondly was also someone who genuinely respected and admired Wilder's innate cinematic skills and his uncanny grasp of the human condition. Paradoxically, he also still liked Billy, even though he really couldn't stand being around him.

It seems abundantly clear that *Ace in the Hole* was precisely the kind of material, slightly soiled, which Brackett would have had no interest in exploring but which Billy hungered for, and which he celebrated in his ex-partner's absence: "We did not agree on much. But what we agreed on was more important than the long list of what we did not agree on. You have to know what you can argue about, safe argument territory. It's a question of something sacred. I wanted to approach different themes, to question things. We just didn't agree with what those themes should be." So he went ahead and explored them on his own, often very insightfully, occasionally not very. By the time of *Ace*, of course, they weren't exactly chatty with each other, so nothing stood in the way of Wilder's appetite for adventurous narratives.

Wilder himself, meanwhile, never one to be self-effacing, had long ago made peace with his own quirky personality and contradictory character structure, admitting that the closing line from one of his most popular later films was the one that embodied his basic ethos as an artist and his attitude as a person: "Nobody's perfect, is the line that most sums up my work. There is no comedy and no drama about perfect people." Therefore, it almost stands to reason, from his perspective, that an artist who makes cultural commentary about everyday people should not himself be exempt from the freedom to be imperfect. He embraced his own imperfection with considerable gusto.

He enjoyed that closing line from *Some Like It Hot* so much, in fact, that he approved of Charlotte Chandler's choice of it as the title for her personal profile of him. Not only that, he also instructed his estate that this short phrase was to be used as the epitaph on his gravestone: "I'm a writer, but then, nobody's perfect." Writing—that was where Chandler's exchanges with the director, which by all accounts were easygoing and amusing affairs (as he was generally often at his most charming and engaging with female interlocutors), began as a point of departure in her profile. Chandler immediately got Wilder into a comfortable and conversational mode when she started exploring his long career with him for her 2002 study of the man and his work.

Wilder, with some amusement, also declared that this most famous movie line of his, and the choice for his gravestone, actually wasn't even his own line but that of his second screenwriting collaborator, I. A. L. Diamond (1920–1988). Known as "Iz" by everyone in the business, Diamond was born Iztek Domnici in Bessarabia, Romania, in what is now Moldova. They proved compatible, perhaps because they were both Jewish, or because they were both émigrés who reinvented themselves in a new world writing dreams that money can buy, or perhaps it was because, like Billy, Iz could also rightly say, "The town where I was born is still there. But the country is gone."

Diamond was a longtime friend of Wilder's who already had a lengthy career of his own in Hollywood when the two began partnering on the writing of what would turn out to be twelve of Wilder's most popular and successful movies. Their acclaimed run commenced with *Some Like It Hot* in 1959 and traversed some sparkling territory, including *The Apartment* (1960), *One, Two, Three* (1961), *Irma la Douce* (1963), *Kiss Me Stupid* (1964), *The Fortune Cookie* (1966), all the way to *Buddy Buddy* (1981), and it included some of Jack Lemmon and Walter Matthau's most memorable screen moments.

"Nobody's perfect, it wasn't even mine. It was Iz's." This salvo permitted Wilder to amuse Chandler with some of his most tried-and-true literary self-interpretations, which by the twenty-first-century appearance of her biography had practically become etched in marble, so often had he used them in interviews such as hers. (Wilder passed away in 2002, the year her book was published). The most familiar echo of his earlier screenwriting partnership with Brackett (with whom he created the same number of films as a team) was his analogy for the craft of writing in tandem: "A good writing collaboration is more difficult to achieve than a good marriage. And it's more intimate." Sound familiar? It was almost identical, word for word, to what he had said about his partnership with Brackett back in 1938.

But he went further than that in the twilight of his career: "Iz was not only my writing partner, but also my alter-Id, my alter-Iz."

One notes with bemusement that this particular partner was not, as the earlier one had been, an alter ego . . . but rather, an *alter id*, perhaps suggesting a comparably primal and bedrock kind of pairing of raw, unbridled desires. "It's important to learn how to fight. You have to be able to argue about something so you don't destroy anything basic about the relationship. You have to be able to come back for more." According to Wilder, Diamond simply ad-libbed that short line, after a long day of exhausting work together, and it rang a little bell in their heads.

Most intriguingly, and as emphasized by Chandler as a key feature of their alter-id-ness, she also went to speak to Diamond, too, and when she told him about Wilder's attributing the famous line to him, he was taken aback. "Oh no," Diamond said. "That's not true. 'Nobody's perfect' was his. It absolutely was *his* line." And as Chandler accurately observed about this blurring of boundaries, "*that* was a collaboration." Wilder had been there before, of course, this intimate kind of pairing—almost a marriage—with another creative person, so he recognized at once what it means to collaborate so seamlessly with a partner that it ends up being unclear whose idea was whose, since in actuality, all of them are *theirs*. After half a century, of course, and while "tiptoeing into the twenty-first century at the age of ninety-four," as Wilder put it, one easily returns to rehearsed and regular routines in order to develop a kind of mnemonic shorthand. But though the concrete details of his earlier collaboration may have faded somewhat into the mists of legend, the lingering pains it left behind still percolated in some deep, submerged place.

As Zolotow described the rancor, the former partners "never forgave each other. Brackett rarely spoke of Wilder. I asked Brackett a question about Billy, he froze up. Wilder, on his part, also spoke as little as possible about his work with Brackett. He wanted to forget Charlie." My obvious question is: why, why did he long so fervently to forget his work with Brackett? Examples are legion. For instance,

Zolotow notes that when *A Foreign Affair* screenwriter Richard Breen collaborated with Brackett, "Wilder cut him off and would not see him socially or work with him professionally." A similar breach occurred with Walter Reisch when he began working with Brackett. But why?

In one of Zolotow's exchanges with Wilder, he confided to him that he often wondered about Garson Kanin's observations in his book *Hollywood*, from 1974, which contained very unflattering images of Wilder as what Zolotow interpreted as "a monster." He asked Wilder about the seventy-five-year-old Brackett's deathbed confidences to Kanin. The response was compelling in its absence: "Wilder stopped pacing. He stared out of a window. Do you know what he said? Nothing. Absolutely nothing. And I changed the subject." It is entirely possible that somewhere in a dim, subterranean chamber inside Wilder, he not only regretted his treatment of Brackett but also, perhaps secretly, realized something had changed drastically in his work.

Sam Staggs has observed that "Brackett's absence from *The Big Carnival (Ace in the Hole)* resonates. . . . Motifs from their scripts recur in film after film, no matter who happens to be Wilder's collaborator. This underlines the great guiding genius of Brackett on his volatile younger partner. As the years go by, the ghost of Charles Brackett's restraining hand seems to stretch toward Wilder, who never accepts the offer." I wholeheartedly agree. Regardless of how popular or successful his later pictures might be, and they clearly garnered much acclaim, something elemental was missing, some nebulous ingredient that only comes along once in a lifetime, if you're lucky. But Billy, it appears, often had luck on his side.

One of the hallmarks of the Wilder career, apart from his extraordinary storytelling and filming acumen, was the ironic mix of totally successful adulation alternating with vigorous panning and eye-rolling. He was especially adept at rolling with the negative criticisms of this or that film, as he passionately believed that the next movie would be another *The Lost Weekend* or *Sunset Boulevard*. But of course, it never was. "A man *is* his achievements," he commented, inadvertently revealing a part of his core belief system and guiding principles. "There's nothing more terrible than to want to ride and not to have a horse. Slumps can't be figured. You're the same person, same abilities. It's the secret element that you can't figure—when your timing, your luck goes off. It happens to ball players, to film directors, even to vineyards. When you want a home run too badly you press and strike out. The problem is the lack of success changes you and you act more defensively, or more desperately, and you hurt your own chance of success."

Unfortunately for Billy, subsequent to the collective recoiling from *Ace in the Hole*—a film which I still maintain is a prophetic masterpiece despite its distasteful aura—he lurched, in my opinion, toward the utterly weird choice of a black comedy set in a German prisoner-of-war camp, something so cinematically depressing that it was practically doomed to become the toxic germ of one of the most offensive network television shows ever created, *Hogan's Heroes*. Luckily, *Stalag 17*, an utterly clueless nostalgia and neurosis mash-up that found Wilder with no one to stop him from returning once again to wartime Germany, was made the year *before* he had another similar screenwriting synchronicity occur, in the form of his propitious encounter with I. A. L. Diamond, whom he would come to regard with an attitude of amor fati. *Stalag 17*, written by Wilder himself and his coauthor Edwin Blum, was a grim film adaptation of an anti-glitzy play on Broadway written by Donald Bevan and Edmund Trzcinski. (Weirdly, Bevan was also the caricaturist for the celebrity wall at Sardi's restaurant in New York for over twenty years.)

I think Staggs is quite correct in his judgment that not only is this film an oddly misbegotten mixture of two genres (World War

II comedy and concentration camp tragedy) squashed together, but "Wilder's second film without the Brackett radar shows him veering further off-course." The most succinct and astute film review ever penned, or certainly the shortest, anyway.

Most tellingly, Paramount held back the release of *Stalag 17* for an entire year, afraid that the public would neither understand nor appreciate a black comedy about prisoners of war. Equally tellingly, it then only decided to put the movie out in 1953 because the North Koreans had released some American prisoners and some suit decided it would be a useful exploitation gimmick. How this decidedly odd context for a film, based on an even more peculiar Broadway show, could ever have been imagined in the first place is revealing psychologically.

It fails for exactly the same reason that *A Foreign Affair*, another political vehicle, succeeded: its clever screenwriting strategy was to situate the film in *postwar* Berlin, thus permitting Wilder and Brackett to approach the Nazi subject from a historical perspective which literally demonstrated the sad outcomes of fascist ideology. The attempt to make light of incarceration was an eccentric one to say the least, almost as eccentric as Wilder's next venture, this time back into romantic comedy, with the equally objectionable *Sabrina* in 1954.

Sabrina, the last film Wilder made for Paramount, ending their phenomenally successful twelve-year business relationship, was expected to be charming fun, and many audiences enjoyed it exactly on those terms despite its heavy-handed clichés. Humphrey Bogart was extremely unhappy with his seducer role, believing himself to be too old to court the sprightly Audrey Hepburn, which he was. That didn't stop him from having a passionate real-life affair with the younger actress, of course, and also having extreme difficulties with both his costar, William Holden, and his director, Wilder, both of whom he appeared to despise.

As a single transitional film for Twentieth Century Fox, the studio his ex-partner Brackett had decamped to after their divorce, and prior to Wilder's own setting up shop at the Warner Brothers studio with a new screenwriting partner, *The Seven Year Itch* was mostly a cheeky vehicle for the splendid charms of Marilyn Monroe and her billowing skirt. But Wilder was not the first member of the esteemed creative team to access the unique aura of Marilyn. That delight befell his former partner Brackett, who would unveil her special vibe in one of the two highly successful films he would produce on his own after their breakup. Meanwhile, Wilder was afloat on a sea of uncertainty, making sincere but lackluster attempts to repeat the glories of *Sunset Boulevard*. To even approach those heights, however, he would need to find, and potentially train, a new screenwriting partner, one who might be willing to do his bidding, while also helping to prevent him from being trapped in a room alone with his typewriter.

Once on the scene, I. A. L. Diamond worked out well as a fresh collaborator, especially since more of a safe social and critical distance protected Wilder from his new writing partner, as he later explained to Cameron Crowe: "We never talked about personal things. That was the beauty of it. It was not a collaboration like with Brackett, where he told me who his dentist is, kind of things that don't belong, you know?" However, his not knowing the details of his partner's life away from the studio office did seem to have something of a bracing effect on what might be called his screenwriting collaboration sequel. His second run at partnership would garner him a Writers Guild of America Award for Career Achievement with Diamond in 1980. It was exactly the same Writers Guild Career Achievement recognition that Wilder had first received, way back in 1957.

Staggs observed ruefully the distinctions to be made between the two partnerships in Wilder's meteoric trajectory: "Fascination, relentless and unshakeable, characterizes the professional marriage of Wilder and Diamond. . . . Wilder's resume, during the first decade after Brackett, reads like a précis of every good Hollywood director's career: eight solid pictures in ten years, a couple not so good, several above average, and two first-rate. Would anyone, even the most fundamentalist auteur critic, equate the twelve Wilder and Diamond pictures with the thirteen of Brackettandwilder?" The answer is obvious.

Paradoxically, Wilder's new film with Diamond co-writing, an atrocious bomb called *Love in the Afternoon* with a tired Gary Cooper and an all-too-exquisitely-nubile Audrey Hepburn, would be released the same year he received the Writers Guild award for his work with his now-absent writing partner. Equally ironic was Diamond's winning the Writers Guild award for Best American Comedy for *Love in the Afternoon*. It does deserve attention for the screenplay and for the film's overall Lubitsch-like vibe. My cranky disdain for it is likely unfair and more rooted in the slightly debauched attraction between Gary and Audrey as it appears in our century rather than how it came across in the middle of the last. Which was basically: everything is A-OK here, nothing to see here. Indeed, there really wasn't.

Have I by any chance given Billy's films short shrift here? I don't think so.

* * *

Why "Coasting Home"? Because that's exactly what both men were doing subsequent to their torrid creative collaboration: sailing confidently, and perhaps more calmly, toward each of their personal homelands stylistically. One moved closer to the comforting light, and one moved closer to the uncomfortable darkness. While Billy was busy being Billy, in 1951 Charlie quickly released a couple of sheer feel-good confections: *The Mating Season*, a farce with some elements of screwball comedy with Gene Tierney and John Lund, and *The Model and the Stockbroker*, a romantic comedy with Jeanne

Crain and Thelma Ritter. Neither went to a place where changes to the history of cinema are located, but then again, he wasn't trying to go to that place; he'd been there already with his former partner, and he wasn't so sure he liked the climate. Time for some fresh iterations of past motifs.

By contrast, Brackett's solo ventures minus Wilder were on much more solid and balanced footing, and in his own voice. His first two major and serious post-Billy films as both producer and co-screenwriter were met with great acclaim. Both arrived hot on the heels of each other in the same year that Wilder's bizarre prison camp comedy unfolded, in many cases before a bewildered audience. In 1953, Brackett won an Academy Award for Best Original Screenplay, for *Titanic*, with a real ship, and was roundly rewarded by favorable criticism for his other fine film that same year, *Niagara*, which should have been taken far more seriously as a late noir classic but was misunderstood, partly because of the stunningly distracting Marilyn Monroe and partly because it was shot in Technicolor. It's quite possible that the Oscar bestowed on Brackett for *Titanic*, shared with his co-writers Richard Breen and Walter Reisch, was the unfortunate cause of Wilder's ill-advised blackballing of those two able writers.

In terms of the kind of both critical and commercial success that might also have rankled the overly competitive and insecure Wilder, Brackett's raking in such glowingly positive accolades for his 1956 musical *The King and I*, for which he was nominated for Best Picture, must have been at the top of Billy's list. Another Oscar nod, this time an Honorary Academy Award for his lifetime contribution to the Motion Picture Arts and Sciences, was tossed Brackett's way in 1958, by which time his trying period of mentoring Billy was a full two decades in the past. Brackett's post-Wilder career was a consistently stellar series of entertaining vehicles which he engineered as a creative producer now unburdened by the constraints of either ego or partnership.

He continued serving as the President of the Academy of Motion Picture Arts and Sciences, where he was liked by all and sundry for his professionalism and his old-fashioned civility. He was also liked by audiences, who flocked to his progressively more big-budget pictures always certain that he would absorb them in engrossing human narratives, but without hitting them over the head with any self-conscious artistry or socially demanding messages. To that extent, he followed the core dictum of a director he wrote for earlier in his career, one whom Wilder despised: Mitchell Leisen, an artist who likewise reserved the rightful place for delivering messages to Western Union. I suppose Wilder didn't get that memo.

Amazingly, the barely three months between the release of Brackett's two remarkable solo ventures in 1953 show that he was undertaking two opening salvos in his post-Wilder career at the same time. But he was of course doing this openly, and not, as it must appear to any observer, secretly, as Wilder had to have been doing during the final months of making *Sunset Boulevard* with Brackett while also furtively planning his grand departure into *Ace in the Hole*.

These two Brackett films, both written by himself with erstwhile collaborators Breen and Reisch, and directed by renowned directors Henry Hathaway and Jean Negulesco, are among the early gems of Brackett's unbridled creativity after the captivity of a claustrophobic and acerbic partnership. And he would be rewarded accordingly, both critically and commercially, releasing three of his best films in rapid succession. Wilder would also be rewarded with three Oscars for his brilliantly biting 1959 and 1960 social satires on contemporary American mores, *Some Like It Hot* and *The Apartment*. Brackett and Wilder had both reached that final, anything-you-can-do-I-can-do-better phase of their respective competitive careers.

Historically now properly identified as an American film noir, at the time *Niagara* was a surprising shift into color (three-strip

Technicolor, prior to Cinemascope), but with so many key dark features thematically I would still call it daylight-noir. This was one of Twentieth Century Fox's biggest box office smashes of the year. Most notably, Marilyn Monroe was given top billing for the film, a designation that elevated her into the star status which would be crystallized by the two other amazing films released in 1953, *Gentlemen Prefer Blondes* and *How to Marry a Millionaire*.

Also notable is the fact that ten years later, Andy Warhol would "borrow" one of Brackett's publicity shots of Marilyn sitting on a wall before Niagara Falls for his important silkscreen painting of the star, *Marilyn Diptych*, shortly after her demise. Here she embodies the femme fatale persona quite literally as she encounters a honeymooning couple at the falls and they become enmeshed in her troubled marriage with a character played by Joseph Cotten, whom she plans to murder with the help of her lover Patrick. Instead, her husband kills the lover and subsequently he strangles her, before attempting to escape in a small boat that is dragged over the falls to his doom. A techie friend of mine created a black-and-white version of *Niagara* for me in order to absorb all of the salient noir overtones that become slightly wayward in the color realm.

Fox head honcho Darryl Zanuck was pleased that his studio scored Monroe as the star for Brackett's film, and Brackett no doubt was pleased that he got to bask in Marilyn's aura two years before his ex-partner Billy would avail himself of her talents in *The Seven Year Itch* and four years later again for *Some Like It Hot*. It irked the writers, however, that this fresh new star was being touted as the murderous villain in the storyline, rather than focusing on her more appealing features. But Marilyn was delighted to undertake a role that toyed with her stereotypes so dramatically.

Variety took exception to veteran Hollywood director Henry Hathaway (best known for shooting classic westerns with John Wayne, Randolph Scott, and Gary Cooper) taking such an ominous dark turn, although audiences loved the whole scenario and its late noir flavors. Their reviewer complained the film was "a morbid, clichéd expedition into lust and murder. The atmosphere throughout is strained and taxes the nerves with a feeling of impending disaster." Exactly what nervous audiences needed to distract them from current events like the Korean War and our potential nuclear annihilation.

Brackett's new storytelling direction was followed only about twelve weeks later by the bombastic *Titanic*, directed by Jean Negulesco. Once again Zanuck had intervened with an idea he had imagined would capitalize on the newly devised widescreen format, inviting Brackett's screenwriting partner Walter Reisch to a meeting and declaring, "I have Clifton Webb under contract, and we now have Cinemascope, so now I want to do something big! Don't make Clifton a clown, I want him to start a new career as a character actor. Use all the young people we have on the lot, like Audrey Dalton and Robert Wagner."

The fact that it was "sixty percent truth and semi-documentary" was reassuring to Zanuck, perhaps, though it also had an abundance of historical inaccuracies: the ship was not sold out, for instance, and the character played by Clifton Webb, searching for the wife and kids who were walking out on him to live in America, could easily have gotten on board. None of that stopped audiences from loving the tale of domestic discord nestled within the arms of a massive historic tragedy, even though, as Pauline Kael snarkily commented, "The actual sinking looks like a nautical tragedy on the pond in Central Park." This small family disaster narrative, lost in the swirl of a huge human catastrophe, won the producer-writer an Academy Award for Best Screenplay, setting Brackett well on his way to successfully leaving behind Billy and all, or most, of his bickering. Working with Negulesco, an accomplished director of such noir classics as *Road House* (1948), *Forbidden Street* (1949), and *Phone Call from a*

Stranger (1952), was an ideal way for Brackett to achieve that desired distance.

In rapid succession, and all before gaining massive acclaim with his next award-winning musical blockbuster, Brackett released *Woman's World* (1954), a corporate drama with Lauren Bacall and Fred MacMurray; *Garden of Evil* (1954), a grand Cinemascope western with Gary Cooper, Susan Hayward, and Richard Widmark; *The Virgin Queen* (1955), a historical Elizabeth drama shot in DeLuxe Color with Bette Davis and Richard Todd; *The Girl in the Red Velvet Swing* (1955), a dramatic romance with Ray Milland and a young Joan Collins; *Teenage Rebel* (1956), touted as a "grown-up motion picture for grown-up emotions," with Ginger Rogers and Michael Rennie; and of course, Brackett's ultimate meditation on et cetera, *The King and I*. Was he attempting to send any deep social messages in these movies? Of course not. He was having a good time and inviting audiences to do the same.

One way of establishing himself as an independent filmmaker, one newly divorced from Billy, would be to craft one of the two or three best musical films Hollywood ever released. Brackett's take on the Anna and King of Siam storyline ranks up there with *West Side Story* and *Oklahoma!* in the genre of musical entertainment. Even though I'm far from being a fan of musicals, despite being a fan of the Irene Dunne version released a decade earlier, I can still recognize when one is watching a masterpiece, especially one which my mother was fond of telling me she saw over 1,200 times as an usherette at the university theater. My own two viewings, however, were more than enough to qualify this emotional extravaganza as a great work of cinema, regardless of genre. I'm just glad I didn't have to be subjected to 1,198 more screenings of it. It was nominated for nine Oscars, among them Best Picture for Brackett, as well as a Best Actor win for Brynner. In all, it won five statues, as well as a Golden Globe Award for Best Picture. The film remains banned in Thailand.

Much has already been written on Wilder's later films, of course, particularly in those fine pages by Billy expert Gene Phillips and Wilder specialist Joseph McBride. For me, his gradual descent followed the same arc as his meteoric ascent, but in reverse. *Witness For the Prosecution* (1957), Wilder's courtroom potboiler that reunited him with Marlene Dietrich and provided a chance to direct the great Tyrone Power and formidable Charles Laughton, was a respectable stepping stone toward his mature career phase. But the director's two true masterpieces of this middle phase of his long, long (almost too long) career are undoubtedly the film that fully formalized Marilyn Monroe as both a bona fide superstar as well as an actress of considerable sensitivity, and then the film the following year that focused our attention for a second time on perhaps our ultimate everyman and dependably nervous Billy-cipher, the multitalented Jack Lemmon.

Obviously the crux of my narrative suggests that more than enough airtime has been devoted to Wilder over the years, and my aim has been to try to give something approaching equal attention to Brackett's contributions, before, during and after Billy. After all, Billy did survive Charlie for another thirty-three years. I also easily accede to the undeniable reality that Wilder was a cinematic genius, but also propose that Brackett didn't just teach him to speak English, he also taught him how to speak American. And although Wilder was a singularly gifted artist, as well as being a supernal control freak, he was never ever one who liked to write or work alone. Toward the end of his life, perhaps growing wistful, if still not exactly friendly, he opined, "If only God would send me another Brackett or Diamond." He apparently couldn't.

And despite all his myriad flaws, or maybe even because of them, as the two decades of his triumph were turning a corner into the tumultuous social and cultural upheaval of 1960s, Wilder would release at least two more of his greatest achievements and most important cultural commentaries. *Some Like It Hot* was released on March 29, 1959. This film, probably Marilyn's apotheosis, practically singlehandedly did away with the Hays Office's censorship controls as a result of its deft handling of cross-dressing and gender flexibility. And *The Apartment*, released June 15, 1960, is one of Wilder's most important films, albeit one of the darkest and most distressing exposes of a misogynistic and superficial social order. For me, it is much more important than his later amusing but trivial buddy movies featuring Lemmon and Matthau, and I also believe it is as prescient and brilliant in its forecasting of the *Mad Men* behavioral era as *Ace in the Hole* was at signaling the frenzied arrival of the new and crass communications era all of us now occupy.

As usual, Billy just got there way ahead of the rest of us.

EPILOGUE

A Mask Made of Mirrors

Want to buy some illusions? Slightly used, second-hand? Some for laughs, some for tears.

MARLENE DIETRICH, IN *A FOREIGN AFFAIR*.

Yes, movies are magic, it's true. It's also true that all filmmakers, almost without exception, are hypersensitive artists capable of great moments of empathy by reflecting our world back to us, even back at us. They also often need to somehow protect themselves personally from our insistent gaze, while still inviting it to be bestowed on their movies. Many of the great ones wear a mask, or persona, behind which they salvage as much of a private life as possible, and that mask, being crafted from mirrors, tends to reflect everything in the environment, including all of us—everything except the filmmaker wearing the mirrored mask. But part of the inherent magic of movies is how easy it is, eventually, to begin to read the films themselves as diaristic documents that archive the ideas or feelings of the person who writes and directs them.

Johnny Mercer's cheeky song from the 1937 film *Hollywood Hotel* comes to mind in this and every other regard: "Hollywood / where any office boy or young mechanic / can be a panic / with just a good-looking pan." Martin Turnbull, the noirish author of a seductive series of linked novels set in the beating heart of old Hollywood, succinctly called the "Garden of Allah" novels, conducts his thriving business of literary historical fiction in an alternate universe with a permanent 1930s/1940s address worth visiting on a regular basis. I interviewed him about the time period he specializes in.

In one of the books in his intriguing Garden of Allah series—book six, *Twisted Boulevard*—the author even uses the template of an ousted MGM screenwriter named Marcus Adler who evokes the Joe Gillis character's attempts to restart his career with a disgraced movie star in *Sunset Boulevard*. But a Hollywood censor reminds him that misdeeds of the past are not soon forgotten, and a *Hollywood Reporter* columnist searching for gossip, Kathryn Massey, finds herself on the set of the film *Sunset Boulevard* and discovers haunting glimpses into her own past while observing the film in progress. Subsequent to it being the actual 1852 Sunset Boulevard residence of silent screen legend Alla Nazimova, who called her notorious playground mansion the Garden of Allah, the Garden of Allah Hotel opened in 1927 just prior to the advent of the talkies, and it closed in 1959 at the end of the Hollywood studio era.

Thus it can quite truthfully be said that the Garden of Allah bore witness to the entire Golden Age of Hollywood. So it struck me that an author with so many characters dwelling in this nostalgic time period must also be spending a lot of time in that era himself, and also that his take on the time in question might be informative. I was right. When I asked him what cinematic frame of reference most qualified as the "Golden Age," and how the studio system, Paramount among others, functioned so much like a well-oiled piece of industrial equipment, and also how the renowned team of Brackett and Wilder, among others, reached a kind of creative stratosphere, he was as insightful as his novels are entertaining: "To my mind, the golden age of film started with the introduction of the talkies, with Crosland's *The Jazz Singer* in 1927, and ended in 1959, with the Wyler blockbuster *Ben-Hur*. You could, perhaps, argue, that Kubrick's *Spartacus* was a big studio movie from the

Golden Age, but it was written by Dalton Trumbo mostly because the producers consciously flew in the face of the Hollywood Blacklist, which I would argue marked the actual start of the end of the studio era."

I'd have to concur with his historical analysis. But even more insightful, for me, was Turnbull's cogent observation about two elements: the secret bond between comedy and tragedy, and the symbiosis of what Arthur Koestler once called the "holarchy," a dynamic link between opposing forces joined in a mutual creative effort.

In doing so, Turnbull also focused my attention on the obscure nature of what this particular stormy partnership was able to accomplish, largely by revealing the intimate connection between distinctly different and conflicting polarities, as well as by demonstrating how spookily comedy *conceals* tragedy beneath a cloak of chuckles. Both styles exist as behavioral extremities. We depend on our own shadow sides to provide us with a full appreciation of what living has to offer. "To my way of thinking," Turnbull surmised, "a screwball comedy is a romantic comedy with the romantic element deemphasized in favor of heightening and exploiting the comedy element, employing plot mechanics like masquerade, mistaken identity, as well as clever and hyperarticulate wordplay." This paradox provides us ample room for laughter in response.

Turnbull continues, "Film noir, on the other hand, explores darker sides of life in which its characters have been dealt a tough hand . . . and are trying to make their way through life by taking shortcuts that the audience knows are likely to get them deeper into trouble. We start watching screwball comedy knowing that it'll have a happy ending, regardless of how real life works, whereas we watch a film noir knowing that while the ending might be downbeat, whatever happens we know will be more like true life."

The question of how two different personalities clashing repeatedly in a small room over a typewriter might bridge insurmountable distances is even more oblique: how to explain the dynamics of two cooperating collaborators whose temperaments are so different that they don't like each other at all, but they still have that strange magic at play when working together? "I can only imagine that they were opposite sides of the same coin, each with qualities that complemented the other. It's been a while since I read the selection of Brackett diaries . . . but I remember thinking that the two men must have *mirrored* their shadow selves to each other. Most people avoid facing their shadow sides, but these two men were smart enough and creative enough to realize that much could be mined from their death-grip dance. I doubt any of this was a conscious act, but anyone who has been in a love-you-hate-you relationship, knows the feeling well enough."

As to the often-debated issue of whether Wilder was a cold-hearted cynic or a disappointed romantic, and how the unhappiest happy couple could possibly have melted into the singularity that is a holarchy, Turnbull again was an informative respondent: "My favorite movie of theirs together is *Sunset Boulevard* because of its perfect concoction of tone, pacing, casting, and cinematography. I don't think a pure coldhearted cynic could have made the variety of movies that Wilder made. If he'd been one of those, we would think of him now as *only* a film noir director." All of which tends to suggest that his shadow, Charles Brackett, was something even more rare: a romantic cynic whose penchant for a wistful and charming survival mechanism allowed him to transform Wilder, via a kind of balsamic reduction of himself, into a dream merchant extraordinaire.

Film critic Manny Farber, already writing about the need for reassessing the talented but troubled team's screen works as early as 1957 in the curiously titled essay "Underground Films" in *Commentary*, was one of those rare clear-eyed assessors of the Brackett-Wilder style canon with the capacity to see beyond the gritty surface they explored and into the depths of feeling lurking underneath. He was active in promoting their edgy attempts to dig deeper, to tunnel beneath the emotional landscapes of their films in order to unearth their frequently very sensitive insights into what we all have come to call the human condition. It was often not a pretty excavation.

As Gene Phillips has also observed about Wilder's reactions to his film community's interpretations of his work, specifically his brilliant *The Apartment*, he was deeply wounded by many in the industry labeling it a "dirty fairy tale." It especially irked him that so many failed to see his frequent representations of some form of redemption: "The picture reflects a belief in human values, set against life in the urban jungle." Wilder saw no conflict between his cynical wit and his hope for humanity, and he commented, "In my opinion, *The Apartment* is a highly moral picture." As usual, and in retrospect, he was so right that it's scary.

The single most salient and perspicacious observation by any Wilder historian I've yet encountered was that made by Joseph McBride in *Dancing on the Edge*: "Wilder was a compulsive entertainer. His work seems so accessible and easily intelligible, so beguiling and ostensibly transparent, yet there are troubling and obscure currents moving under its surface that have remained largely unexplored. . . . Beneath what seem the shadowy realms of his artistic personality are 'the phantoms of the past,' in the words of a song performed by Marlene Dietrich in *A Foreign Affair*."

Chief among the attributes coming into focus for the peripatetic filmmaker is his inability to ever simply slow down or *stop*. He was clearly driven. But what was it that drove him so relentlessly? Later, his alter ego Jack Lemmon would remark that "Wilder was a live wire, he was a foot and a half off the ground and he had everybody else a foot and a half off the ground all day long with his energy level. I think if there's a picture of him sitting down it must be in the Smithsonian—I don't know, I've never seen one." But, of course, it's highly probable that his buzzing vibe also had to do with the speed-drenched uppers he was always popping on set to keep up his frenzied workload.

I. A. L. Diamond, the screenwriter who replaced Charles Brackett in Wilder's creative affections, had an intimate proximity to the torrent of thoughts that would tumble out of Wilder's lips, often before his mind had finished fully forming them into actual language. "Billy was too restless to sit at a typewriter," he recalled. His generous cohort would concur, while Diamond's son Paul, also a screenwriter himself, was perhaps more accurate, if slightly blunt, when he shared of Wilder that "Sharks don't sleep. They have to keep on moving."

Ironically, his restless movements were initiated involuntarily with his exile from Europe to America, but subsequently his perpetual motion strategy seems to have been developed as a survival mechanism. As McBride points out in *Dancing on the Edge*, "Wilder's habitual feeling of being *ausländisch* (foreign or alien) deeply influenced his work as a filmmaker. . . . Even after becoming more secure in his success, he remained a perpetual outsider at heart, always conscious of his marginality." Surely that word, *ausländisch*, has a direct link to our word outlandish? And the link was brought home all the more clearly recently when a cinematic friend of mine admitted that even though he agreed with me that not all of Wilder's later films were sterling, and that he too didn't admire *all* of his work, there was more than enough sheer *oomph* to his artistic gifts to cause him to declare of Wilder, "Well, he was just outlandishly talented, wasn't he?" Yes, he was.

Subsequent to 1960—a kind of watershed point in both their careers, it seems to me—both of the artists under consideration embarked on their own creative binges, each indulging in his own customary notions, captivating stories, and idiosyncratic images. In Wilder's case, *One, Two, Three*, a 1961 frenetic comedy of manners with James Cagney; *Irma la Douce*, a strangely depressing vehicle for the wonderfully sad Shirley MacLaine, also in 1961; and *The Fortune*

Cookie, his last formulaic farce of the decade with his new alter egos, Lemmon and Matthau, in 1966, are all able entertainments and iterations of his tried-and-true social-satire scenarios. But in his final decade of moviemaking, from 1970's *Private Life of Sherlock Holmes* (butchered by studio interventions), 1972's *Avanti*, and 1974's *The Front Page*, culminating in 1978's *Fedora* and 1981's *Buddy Buddy*, we do find the master from the Golden Age encountering some rare tarnishing of his legend.

Brackett's version of coasting home, and also of a creative binge, was of course far more benign and much less caustic in its embrace of a new decade with startlingly fresh new social attitudes. It's important to remember how much of a card-carrying Republican Brackett was, after all; the closeted guy did support Barry Goldwater in 1964. Perhaps feeling himself to be a relic of a fast-vanishing and more conservative epoch, he contented himself with providing sheer straightforward entertainment, whether comedic or dramatic, and a welcome diversion from the shock of the new then sweeping across America and the rest of world. He is possibly a living embodiment of the French playwright Racine's astute observation, "Life is a comedy to those who think, and a tragedy to those who feel."

The accomplished essayist Guy Davenport reminds us that some of the most misunderstood satirists—such as the witty ironist Franz Kafka, so often construed as a glum fatalist—were actually extremely funny, both in real life and in their insightfully pessimistic prose. Davenport's *The Comic Muse* goes so far as to hope, "Some genius of a critic will one day show us how comic a writer Kafka is, how a sense of the ridiculous very kin to that of Sterne and Beckett informs all his work. Like Kierkegaard, he saw the absurdity of life as the most meaningful clue to its elusive vitality. His humor authenticates his seriousness."

I would also add the irascible Wilder to the list of such unique humorists, and hazard to say that if Kafka or Kierkegaard had been moviemakers, they might resemble Billy's tone of voice to a surprising degree. Davenport also elucidates some of the paradoxes that abound between the comic and the tragic when he observes, "We trust seriousness to be the firm ground beneath our feet while knowing full well that it is ultimately dull and probably inhuman. . . . We have had Swifts and Juvenals who could hack at the stupidities seriousness thrives on. Their weapon, or tool, is satire, which at its best is actionable. . . . Satire's little sister, comedy, was civilized quite early and given the run of the house. . . . Satire is sneaky, unfair and takes no prisoners. . . . Comedy is a free spirit, full of fun, and has no intention of explaining herself."

The late German author and essayist W. G. Sebald, one of my favorite peripheral visionaries, provided me with a memorable observation, almost casually in passing, about the impermanent vagaries of films as both art and history, whether they are happy or sad, in one of his essays titled "Kafka Goes to the Movies": "Films, far more than books, have a way of disappearing not just from the market but from our memory, never to be seen again. But one remembers some of them even decades later." Such an awareness of the mutability of our memory and also of the fragile nature of the rapid industry of cinema caused me to reflect on why it is that certain films (different ones for every person, of course) will always remain with us as permanent markers of some life-changing event. Such an awareness haunts me in my recollection of the films of Charles Brackett and Billy Wilder, almost as if they had been tattooed onto my imagination.

Now, I'm the first to admit that my response to some of their greatest movies, such as *Ninotchka*, *The Lost Weekend*, and *Sunset Boulevard*, and also to Billy's most brilliant solo ventures such as *Ace in the Hole* and *The Apartment*, is primarily ekphrastic in nature. Ekphrasis—it's a fancy-sounding Greek name for something rather simple but still moving: the sensation of being so impactfully gripped by a work of art, usually a visual piece, that it prompts unsought-after poetic responses. Such flights of fancy create whole pieces which are ancillary to the original inspiring work. One might even call them the satisfaction of an urge to wax rhapsodic in our reactions to the vivid stories they shared with us in the dark. Therefore, I readily accept in myself the origin of such flights in an emotional reaction to a certain film, or even to a single scene in such a film.

One filmmaker friend, Kirk Tougas, has been most helpful in accessing the inner sanctum of how and why films are produced in the first place, and also how they convey to us contemporary evocations of rather ancient and even ritualistic practices. Tougas reminded me of the deep bond that ties comedy and tragedy together, one that originates in the double-barreled wisdom of both Aristotle and Nietzsche. The latter went the furthest in clarifying for us the core irony that would, eventually, be active in the work of binary artists such as Billy Wilder and Charles Brackett, even without ever having watched a film.

And Tougas also reminded me of the sibling status of the two forms of expression: "Comedy highlights the ridiculous and absurd, whether in culture, romance, or especially in taboos. Whereas tragedy emphasizes the deep delusions embedded in self-absorption and hubris. One could say that comedy is about the group and tragedy is about the solitary suffering self. Wilder's *The Apartment* is a lovely mockery of two-faced corporate folk and their sexual duplicity, it's about the bumbling everyman character of Jack Lemmon, and his having to choose between his business world and the lowly working woman whose menial job, that of elevating the high-minded to their phony heights, conceals the actual reality of womanhood."

Nietzsche, of all people, also serves as a threshold one needs to cross over in order to access the mysteries of collaborative ventures such as the pair of polar opposites making the movies we have been examining. "The continuous development of art," Friedrich explained prior to going bonkers, early on in his *The Birth of*

Tragedy, "is bound up with the Apollonian and Dionysian duality.
. . . Through Apollo and Dionysius, the two artful deities, we come to
recognize that their world existed in a tremendous opposition. These
two different tendencies . . . continually incite each other to new and
more powerful births, which perpetuate an antagonism, only super-
ficially reconciled by the common term 'art.'"

At the risk of bending scholarship completely out of shape, or
perhaps rather to adopt a kind of aesthetic origami in order to do
so, I would surmise that Charles Brackett represented the Apollonian side of their partnership equation, devoted to order, decorum,
logic, and discourse, while Billy Wilder channeled the more Dionysian side of the ledger, being more committed to disruption, discord,
mayhem, and dance. The balance sheet between these two distant
poles, however, was sufficient to give birth to a work of art as stylistically and socially biting as *Sunset Boulevard*.

I must admit that I do also find a similar form bending to be quite
appealing, and that is the notion that the films of this pair, and even
the films they made after their equation fell apart, uncannily resemble certain traits usually associated with other art forms, especially
writing and painting: the palimpsest and the pentimento. The first
is a manuscript on which the original writing has been effaced to
make room for writing of a later period, but on which traces of the
original still remain, in a vestigial manner, as something reused or
altered but still recalling its earlier form. The second is a painting
term, where the presence or emergence of earlier images, forms, or
strokes have been changed, enhanced, or merely painted over, leaving ghostly echoes.

I mean this quirky medium-bending strictly in a thematic sense,
with the best examples being the fact that the vibe of *Ninotchka* recurs
in *Ball of Fire* two years later. Likewise, some of the themes in *Ball of
Fire* recur later in Billy's *Some Like It Hot*, while some aspects of *The
Major and the Minor* recur, strangely enough, in Brackett's *The King*

and I. These are faint echoes, admittedly, maybe even totally unconscious on the part of the filmmakers, and yet one can even detect an overlap thematically between Billy's first solo masterpiece, *Ace in the Hole*, and his later dark noir effort, *The Apartment*. (No one will ever convince me that this grimy film gem was solely a comedy.)

Brackett, like Wilder, was equally melancholic and always doing something of a balancing act between these two extremes of self-expression, laughter, and tears, although unlike Wilder, he seemed to have had little to no interest in laying bare the flaws and foibles of the human soul. I suspect that like most introverted intellectuals, he rather liked keeping that spiritual and emotional arm-wrestling match under wraps. In quick succession, his binge produced such wildly varied vehicles for escapism as *The Wayward Bus* (1957), notable mostly for the pairing of Dan Dailey with Jayne Mansfield, as it deconstructs a John Steinbeck story; *Gift of Love* (1958), a torrid melodrama with Lauren Bacall and Robert Stack, on whom the studio must have figured they could capitalize by replicating their chemistry from the earlier Douglas Sirk extravaganza *Written on the Wind*; and *Ten North Frederick* (1958), an attempt to reap more critical rewards by combining Gary Cooper with a steamy John O'Hara novel.

Brackett's binge really kicked into gear in 1959, with three films released in that single year: Clifton Webb's bigamist in *The Remarkable Mr. Pennypacker*; a rather daring examination of teen pregnancy, *Blue Denim*, with Macdonald Carey and featuring Brandon deWilde in his first "adult" role; and the weirdly alluring (if you're ten years old) *Journey To the Center of the Earth*, with the warped pairing of James Mason with Pat Boone and my favorite redhead of all time, Arlene Dahl. He then crashed headlong into a decade he would never be able to accurately depict, let alone survive, with 1960's *High Time*, featuring Bing Crosby going back to college and encountering Tuesday Weld and Fabian, and 1962's farewell to all that, a forced funfest called *State Fair*, stiffly directed by an equally out-of-place José Ferrer and colliding together the incongruous flock of Ann-Margret, Pamela Tiffin, Tom Ewell, Alice Faye, Wally Cox, and Bobby Darin, with a young Marvin Aday, a.k.a. Meat Loaf, as an extra.

The films each man made toward the end of their independent careers only goes to illustrate how vital their earlier creative collaboration had been to both partners. Their twilights also demonstrated something of what was missing in their private ventures apart: the strange magic inherently embodied in that unnerving game of double solitaire in which they had mutually participated. McBride's *Dancing on the Edge* confirms the intuition of many of us about the seismic impact of the collision between the two screenwriters so early in the notorious director's emergence, as well as the pivotal place of Brackett in their ascent together.

Wilder later said he felt more like a grateful immigrant than an exile in the end, although that didn't stop him from skewering the pretensions of his adopted nation any more than it prevented him from shooting the same satirical darts at his native homeland for target practice. As McBride put it, "The unsettled condition of exile was to varying degrees familiar, at times strangely comforting, and often hazardous. The constant role-playing in his films, penchant for themes of masquerade, and precarious blend of comedy and drama are reflections of his ability to cope with such uncertainties. Wilder's work, with its affinities for danger and breaking boundaries, is always dancing on the edge, his characters poised between self-destruction and redemption. . . . It was only when Wilder was fortuitously teamed with Brackett that he was able to escape the straitjacket of his first decades in two countries with very different political systems but depressingly similar film industries."

The characterization of Wilder's new mentor in all things Yank was always almost unanimous among industry players and observers, as McBride notes: "Brackett was known in Hollywood for his urbane craftsmanship, genteel demeanor, collegial diplomatic skills and WASPish emotional reserve. His personality sharply contrasted with that of Wilder, the European Jew from modest origins who restlessly survived several successive exiles to rise to the top in Hollywood through sheer talents and survival skills." But the friendly male-bonding profile in *Life* magazine that had made them both famous was also hugely mythical already, and myths do tend to linger.

It is always a challenge to plumb the depths of such symbiotic relationships and creatively combustible equations. However, there are multiple parallels between them, mostly centering on lifelong insecurities. In Wilder's case it was often projected through his well-known love of masquerade and impersonation, made palpable by his ongoing outsider status as a furtive exile living by cunning and guile. In Brackett's case it was his probable gay or bisexual orientation in an industry not yet known for the acceptance of differing sexualities.

Thus, there could be perceived in both men, in tandem, a basic need to engage in a certain amount of role-playing in order to simply get by on a day-to-day basis. McBride's assessment of the wonderment of a successful team is most instructive when viewed through the lens of this shared discomfort: "Collaborations are always somewhat mysterious, especially in the film world, in which the written record of what actually goes on between people is often scant, and memories are notoriously malleable. Often, even the participants can't truly answer questions of who was responsible for what."

Indeed, often the most accurate answer is not either/or but both, and those engaged in critical studies of such participating players who hope to clearly define the roles of each one is often what McBride described as "quixotic." Fortunately, unlike the mandate of formal biographers, we are more focused on a biography of their competitive fuel together rather than merely on the personal details of their lives. The sublimation of two people into one is almost a psychological effort more than a straightforward narrative one. While is quite true that, in McBride's words, enduring films are "those in which one personality has the dominant vision," it has been my experience that dinergy and synergy, the ability to *take turns* being dominant, were what most ensured the success of this alluring team.

One of the most exotic manifestations of this curious and rare combination of luck and fate is the alchemy of the outsider and what he brings to the new land he is considering colonizing, just as the film colony took root in Hollywood when the twentieth century was barely a year old. To his great credit, Wilder stubbornly resisted any attempts to turn him into a stereotype, the studios' fetishized émigré, and there were many attempts to do so. His resistance seems to have taken the form of a dogged determination to assimilate into the American bloodstream. McBride accurately calls Wilder a perfect example of a "chameleon personality" in his strategy of being as useful as possible to the arcane studio cult edifice he encountered, while at the same time rehearsing his campaign to control the rate at which the American bloodstream pumped, using the movies he would make as his instrument. Commanding the English language first, he surmised, would surely make the next steps more sprightly. When he accepted the Life Achievement Award from the American Film Institute, among the other prerequisite players he graciously mentioned, Wilder also wistfully thanked "Charles Brackett, who desperately tried to help me improve my English."

As I have implied throughout this reflection on a powerful but pathological partnership, it seems clear that Wilder was a deracinated storyteller, one who was uprooted from his natural, geographical, social, and cultural environment. It is telling that this brilliant filmmaker did not ever seem to transcend that status; indeed, he appears to have made a career out of representing displacement in general and his own in particular. He could not, of course, ever really go home again, since his home no longer really existed, so he remained content to re-create a home in his head, one over which he was the sole ruler.

Paradoxically, and from an entirely different angle of approach, Brackett too was a deracinated storyteller, but in his case his exile was from the privileged East Coast literary establishment he gave up on in order to move among the crass geniuses of Hollywood entertainment circles. His displacement, ultimately a highly personal and intimate one, was from his own sexuality, challenged to thrive in the homophobic culture of Hollywood. Both men were outsiders; both were exiles of a different sort.

In the final analysis, there can be no absolutely final analysis: this historic filmmaking team was so otherworldly, and so much of a jigsaw puzzle, that often one can't tell which fragmented piece belongs to which player. But Wilder, for his part, at least, seemed to have achieved a modicum of contentment when he remarked to Charlotte Chandler, "I do not wish I had something else out of myself, it's a life I look back on fondly. I have had a good career, which I have enjoyed. I have done some good work and entertained a few people. Even the suffering I enjoyed." Meanwhile, Charles Brackett's nearly last dying words, those addressed to Garson Kanin about his onetime partner, are also very telling indeed: "I never really knew what happened, I never understood it. Don't you think it was odd what he did?"

Yes, I agree, it was odd. But then what wasn't odd about their entire story? Then I recalled a quote from a favorite poet of mine, W. H. Auden, one that seemed to shed some light on this compelling enigma: "Every man carries with him through life a mirror, one as unique and impossible to get rid of as his own shadow." That also prompted an unsolicited memory of another pair of cinematic partners, and the moment when composer Bernard Herrmann, composer of the scores to many great Alfred Hitchcock movies, tried to quell the storm of his own contentious relationship with the director with the quirky quip, "You know, Hitch, you can't outrun your own shadow." The idea here being that on rare occasions we actually do encounter our own mirror image and shadow in life, embodied in another person, and even more rarely, we somehow end up partnering with them to make something together that we couldn't quite ever quite make separately.

That could be both and blessing and a curse, one that calls to mind the speculations about identity and projection made by Arthur Koestler in the late work he termed a "summing-up." In his last book, *Janus*, he ventured out on an enticing limb, one that might offer some clarity in our attempt to grasp the slippery dynamics of creative genius when it is shared so intimately with someone else. Invoking Donne's poetic insight about the vagaries of imaginary solitude, Koestler launched into his summing-up: "No man is an island: he is a *holon*. Like Janus, the two-faced Roman god, holons have a dual tendency to behave as quasi-independent *wholes*, asserting their individualities, but at the same time act as integrated parts of a larger whole in multi-leveled hierarchies."

And in our case, the whole was a truly unique creative partnership known as *brackettandwilder*, and it gave rise to multiple works of cinematic art of the highest order. Their risky game of double solitaire worked wonders, until it didn't anymore, further revealing that this polarity between the self-assertive and integrative tendencies is a characteristic that preserves order and stability and can only prevail when the two tendencies are in equilibrium. After their fraught experience crafting *Sunset Boulevard*, they weren't. As Koestler observed, in a manner that spookily applies to such cases of precarious détente, "If one of them dominates the other, this delicate balance is disturbed, and pathological conditions of various types make their appearance."

Although that author was not referring to the making of films by two gifted writers merging their talents and resources, it's perfectly applicable to both Brackett and Wilder, together and apart, just as it is to stellar structural units like The Beatles, and the dissolution dynamic is also precisely the same. With movies, of course, we're dealing with the additional subtle fact that a screenwriter, producer, and director are often somewhat secretive personalities who conceal their own natures behind an mirrored mask for their own self-protection, reflecting the society around them in their films. But if we look closely we can perceive the ironic fact that the stories they tell, and the characters they employ to do the job, both reveal almost as much about the artists themselves as it does about the actors on the screen. Maybe even more. And maybe it was accurate after all, that soulful Marvin Gaye song lyric, in this collaborative context: "It takes two, baby / to make a dream come true."

FILMOGRAPHY

BRACKETT AND WILDER JOINT PROJECTS

Bluebeard's Eighth Wife (1938)
Paramount Pictures. Released March 23, 1938. Directed by Ernst
Lubitsch. Screenplay by Charles Brackett and Billy Wilder. Cinema-
tography by Leo Tover. Edited by William Shea. Music by Werner
Heymann. Cast: Claudette Colbert, Gary Cooper, Edward Everett
Horton, David Niven, Franklin Pangborn, Elizabeth Patterson. 85
minutes.

Ninotchka (1939)
Paramount Studios. Released November 9, 1939. Directed by Ernst
Lubitsch. Screenplay by Charles Brackett and Billy Wilder, with Wal-
ter Reisch, from a story by Melchior Lengyel. Cinematography by
William Daniels. Edited by Gene Ruggiero. Music by Werner Hey-
mann. Cast: Greta Garbo, Melvyn Douglas, Ina Claire, Bela Lugosi,
Sig Ruman. 110 minutes.

Midnight (1939)
Paramount Pictures. Released March 15, 1939. Directed by Mitchell
Leisen. Screenplay by Charles Brackett and Billy Wilder. Story by
Edwin Mayer and Franz Schulz. Cinematography by Charles Lang.
Edited by Doane Harrison. Music by Frederick Hollander. Cast:
Claudette Colbert, Don Ameche, John Barrymore, Francis Lederer,
Mary Astor, Elaine Barrie. 94 minutes.

Arise My Love (1940)

Paramount Pictures. Released November 8, 1940. Directed by Mitchell Leisen. Screenplay by Charles Brackett and Billy Wilder, with Jacques Thery, from a story by Benjamin Glazer. Cinematography by Charles Lang, Edited by Doane Harrison. Music by Victor Young. Cast: Claudette Colbert, Ray Milland, Walter Abel, Dennis O'Keefe. 100 minutes.

Hold Back the Dawn (1941)

Paramount Pictures. Released September 26, 1941. Directed by Mitchell Leisen. Screenplay by Charles Brackett and Billy Wilder, with Richard Maibaum and Manuel Reachi, from a 1940 novel by Ketti Frings. Cinematography by Leo Tover. Edited by Doane Harrison. Music by Victor Young. Cast: Olivia de Havilland, Paulette Goddard, Charles Boyer, Walter Abel, Rosemary DeCamp. Narrated by Charles Boyer. 116 minutes.

Ball of Fire (1941)

Paramount Pictures. Released December 2, 1941. Directed by Howard Hawks, Screenplay by Charles Brackett and Billy Wilder, based on the story "From A to Z" by Thomas Monroe and Billy Wilder. Cinematography by Gregg Toland, Edited by Daniel Mandell. Music by Alfred Newman. Cast: Barbara Stanwyck, Gary Cooper, Oskar Homolka, Dana Andrews, Henry Travers. 111 minutes.

The Major and the Minor (1942)

Paramount Pictures. Released September 16, 1942, Produced by Arthur Hornblow Jr. Directed by Billy Wilder. Screenplay by Charles Brackett and Billy Wilder, "as suggested by" a story by Edward Childs Carpenter and Fanny Kilborne. Cinematography by Leo Tover. Edited by Doane Harrison. Music by Robert Dolan. Cast: Ginger Rogers, Ray Milland, Rita Johnson, Robert Benchley, Edward Fleming, Norma Varden. 100 minutes.

Five Graves to Cairo (1943)
Paramount Pictures. Released May 4, 1943. Directed by Billy Wilder. Produced by Charles Brackett and B. G. DeSylva, Screenplay by Charles Brackett and Billy Wilder, based on *Hotel Imperial*, a 1917 Hungarian play by Lajos Biro. Cinematography by John Seitz. Edited by Doane Harrison. Music by Miklos Rozsa. Cast: Franchot Tone, Anne Baxter, Akim Tamiroff, Erich von Stroheim, Peter van Eyck, Fortunio Bonanova. 96 minutes.

Double Indemnity (1944)
Paramount Pictures. Released July 3, 1944. Directed by Billy Wilder, Produced by Joseph Sistrom, Screenplay by Raymond Chandler and Billy Wilder, based on the 1943 novel by James M. Cain. Cinematography by John Seitz. Edited by Doane Harrison. Music by Miklos Rozsa. Cast: Barbara Stanwyck, Fred MacMurray, Edward G. Robinson, Porter Hall, Jean Heather, Byron Burr, Richard Gaines, John Philliber. 107 minutes.

The Lost Weekend (1945)
Paramount Pictures. Released November 29, 1945. Directed by Billy Wilder. Produced by Charles Brackett, Screenplay by Charles Brackett and Billy Wilder, based on the 1944 novel *The Lost Weekend* by Charles Jackson. Cinematography by John Seitz. Edited by Doane Harrison. Music by Miklos Rozsa. Cast: Ray Milland. Jane Wyman, Phillip Terry, Howard da Silva, Doris Dowling, Frank Faylen. 101 minutes.

A Foreign Affair (1948)
Paramount Pictures. Released on June 30, 1948. Directed by Billy Wilder. Produced by Charles Brackett. Screenplay by Charles Brackett, Billy Wilder, Richard Breen, and Robert Harari. Story by David Shaw. Cinematography by Charles Lang. Edited by Doane Harrison. Music by Friedrich Hollaender. Cast: Marlene Dietrich, Jean Arthur, John Lund. 116 minutes.

The Emperor Waltz (1948)
Paramount Pictures. Released on May 26, 1948. Directed by Billy Wilder. Produced by Charles Brackett. Screenplay by Charles Brackett and Billy Wilder. Cinematography by George Barnes. Edited by Doane Harrison. Music by Victor Young. Cast: Bing Crosby, Joan Fontaine, Roland Culver, Lucile Watson, Richard Haydn. 106 minutes.

Sunset Boulevard (1950)
Paramount Pictures. Released August 10, 1950. Directed by Billy Wilder. Produced by Charles Brackett. Screenplay by Charles Brackett, Billy Wilder, and D. M. Marshman. Cinematography by John Seitz. Edited by Doane Harrison and Arthur Schmidt. Music by Franz Waxman. Cast: Gloria Swanson, William Holden, Erich von Stroheim, Nancy Olsen, Fred Clark, Lloyd Gough, Jack Webb, along with Buster Keaton, Hedda Hopper, Sidney Skolsky, Anna Nilsson, H. B. Warner, Henry Wilcoxon, Cecil B. DeMille. 110 minutes.

BRACKETT SOLO PROJECTS

The Uninvited (1944)
Paramount Pictures. Released February 10, 1944, Directed by Lewis Allen. Associate-produced by Charles Brackett. Screenplay by Dodie Smith and Frank Patros, based on the 1941 novel *Uneasy Freehold* by Dorothy Macardle. Cinematography by Charles Lang. Edited by Doane Harrison. Music by Victor Young. Cast: Ray Milland, Ruth Hussey, Donald Crisp, Cornelia Skinner, Gail Russell. 98 minutes.

To Each His Own (1946; co-screenwriter and producer)

Miss Tatlock's Millions (1948; co-screenwriter and producer)

The Mating Season (1951; co-screenwriter and producer)

The Model and the Marriage Broker (1951; co-screenwriter and producer)

Niagara (1953)
Twentieth Century Fox. Released January 21, 1953. Directed by Henry Hathaway. Produced by Charles Brackett. Written by Charles Brackett, Richard Breen, and Walter Reisch. Cinematography by Joseph MacDonald. Edited by Barbara McLean. Music by Sol Kaplan. Cast: Marilyn Monroe, Joseph Cotten, Jean Peters, Max Showalter. Narrated by Joseph Cotton. 88 minutes.

Titanic (1953)
Twentieth Century Fox. Released April 16, 1953. Directed by Jean Negulesco. Produced by Charles Brackett. Written by Charles Brackett, Richard Breen, and Walter Reisch. Cinematography by Joseph MacDonald. Edited by Louis Loeffler. Music by Sol Kaplan. Cast: Barbara Stanwyck, Clifton Webb, Robert Wagner, Audrey Dalton. 98 minutes.

Garden of Evil (1954; producer)

Woman's World (1954; producer)

The Virgin Queen (1955; producer)

The Girl in the Red Velvet Swing (1955; co-screenwriter and producer)

D-Day the Sixth of June (1956; producer)

The King and I (1956)
Twentieth Century Fox. Released June 28, 1956. Directed by Walter Lang. Produced by Charles Brackett. Screenplay by Ernest Lehman, based on the story by Margaret Landon, the memoir of Anna Leonowens, and the Broadway musical play by Rodgers and

Hammerstein. Cinematography by Leon Shamroy. Edited by Robert Simpson. Music by Richard Rodgers. Cast: Deborah Kerr, Yul Brynner, Rita Moreno, Martin Benson, Rex Thompson. 133 minutes.

Teenage Rebel (1956; co-screenwriter and producer)

The Wayward Bus (1957; producer)

The Gift of Love (1958; producer)

Ten North Frederick (1958; producer)

The Remarkable Mr. Pennypacker (1959; producer)

Blue Denim (1959; producer)

Journey to the Center of the Earth (1959; co-screenwriter and producer)

High Time (1960; producer)

State Fair (1962; producer)

WILDER SOLO PROJECTS

Ace in the Hole (1951)
Paramount Pictures. Released June 14, 1951. Produced and directed by Billy Wilder. Screenplay by Billy Wilder, Walter Newman, and Lesser Samuels, from a story by Victor Desney. Cinematography by Charles Lang. Edited by Arthur Schmidt. Music by Hugo Friedhofer. Cast: Kirk Douglas, Jan Sterling, Robert Arthur, Porter Hall. 111 minutes.

The Seven Year Itch (1955)
Twentieth Century Fox. Released June 3, 1955. Directed by Billy Wilder. Produced by Charles K. Feldman and Billy Wilder. Screenplay by George Axelrod and Billy Wilder, based on the 1952 play by

George Axelrod. Cinematography by Milton R. Krasner. Edited by Hugh S. Fowler. Music by Alfred Newman. Cast: Marilyn Monroe, Tom Ewell, Sonny Tufts, Evelyn Keyes, Robert Strauss. 105 minutes.

The Spirit of St. Louis (1957; co-screenwriter and director)

Love in the Afternoon (1957; co-screenwriter, producer, and director)

Witness for the Prosecution (1957; co-screenwriter and director)

Some Like it Hot (1959)
United Artists. Released March 29, 1959. Directed by Billy Wilder. Produced by Billy Wilder. Screenplay by Billy Wilder and I. A. L. Diamond, from a story by Robert Thoeren and Michael Logan. Cinematography by Charles Lang. Edited by Arthur Schmidt. Music by Adolph Deutsch. Cast: Marilyn Monroe, Tony Curtis, Jack Lemmon, George Raft, Joe E. Brown, Pat O'Brien. 121 minutes.

The Apartment (1960)
United Artists. Released June 15, 1960. Directed by Billy Wilder. Produced by Billy Wilder. Screenplay by Billy Wilder and I. A. L. Diamond. Cinematography by Joseph LaShelle. Edited by Daniel Mandell. Music by Adolph Deutsch. Cast: Jack Lemmon, Fred Mac-Murray, Shirley MacLaine, Ray Walston, Edie Adams. 121 minutes.

One, Two, Three (1961; co-screenwriter, producer, and director)

Irma la Douce (1963; co-screenwriter, co-producer, and director)

Kiss Me, Stupid (1964; co-screenwriter, producer, and director)

The Fortune Cookie (1966; co-screenwriter, producer, and director)

The Private Life of Sherlock Holmes (1970; co-screenwriter, co-producer, and director)

Avanti! (1972; co-screenwriter, co-producer, and director)

The Front Page (1974; co-screenwriter and director)

Fedora (1978; co-screenwriter, producer, and director)

Buddy Buddy (1981; co-screenwriter and director)

BIBLIOGRAPHY

Bellwoar, Rachel. "For Your (Re)consideration: Lubitsch's *Bluebeard's Eighth Wife* Reviewed." Comicon.com, May 21, 2020.

Brooks, Peter. *The Melodramatic Imagination and the Mode of Excess.* Yale University Press, 1976.

Cardullo, Bert. *Regarding the Cinema: Fifteen Filmmakers.* Chaplin Books, 2012.

Chadwick, Whitney. *Significant Others.* Thames & Hudson, 1993.

Chandler, Charlotte. *Nobody's Perfect: Billy Wilder—A Personal Biography.* Simon & Schuster, 2002.

Corrigan, Robert. *Comedy: Meaning and Form.* Chandler Publishing, 1965.

Crowe, Cameron. *Conversations with Wilder.* Knopf, 2001.

Dessem, Matthew. *The Rise and Fall of Hollywood's Happiest Couple.* The Dissolve, June 26, 2014

Dickos, Andrew. *Street with No Name: A History of the Classic American Film Noir.* University Press of Kentucky, 2021

Doane, Mary Ann. *The Desire to Desire: The Woman's Film in the 1940s.* Indiana University Press, 1987.

Gemünden, Gerd. *Continental Strangers: German Exile Cinema, 1933–1951.* Columbia University Press, 2014.

———. *A Foreign Affair: Billy Wilder's American Films.* Berghahn Books, 2008.

Harvey, James. *Romantic Comedy in Hollywood: From Lubitsch to Sturges.* Knopf, 1987.

Horton, Robert. *Interviews with Billy Wilder.* University Press of Mississippi, 2001.

John-Steiner, Vera. *Creative Collaboration*. Oxford University Press, 2000.

Karnick, Kristine. *Classical Hollywood Comedy*. Routledge, 1995.

Kehr, Dave. "New DVDs: Mitchell Leisen and 'The Big Trail.'" *The New York Times*, May 13, 2008.

Kolker, Robert. *Film, Form, and Culture*. McGraw-Hill Publishing, 1999.

Koury, Phil. "The Happy Union of Brackett and Wilder." *The New York Times*, April 18, 1948.

Luft, Herbert. "Two Views of Wilder." *Hollywood Quarterly*, 1952.

McBride, Joseph. *Billy Wilder: Dancing on the Edge*. Columbia University Press, 2021.

Melville, David. "Mitchell Leisen." *Senses of Cinema* 37, 2006.

Nugent, Frank. "The Screen in Review; Gary Cooper Comes a Cropper in 'Bluebeard's Eighth Wife.'" *The New York Times*, March 24, 1938.

Park, James. *Learning to Dream*. Faber and Faber, 1984.

Phillips, Gene. *Some Like it Wilder: The Life and Controversial Films of Billy Wilder*. University of Kentucky Press, 2010.

Rappaport, Mark. "Mitchell Leisen." *Rouge* volume 12, 2008.

Sikov, Ed. *On Sunset Boulevard: The Life and Times of Billy Wilder*. Hyperion, 1999.

Silver, Alain and James Ursini. *Film Noir Reader*. Limelight, 1996.

Slide, Anthony, ed. *It's the Pictures That Got Small: Charles Brackett on Billy Wilder and Hollywood's Golden Age*. Columbia University Press, 2015.

Smedley, Nick. *A Divided World: Hollywood Cinema and Émigré Directors in the Era of Roosevelt and Hitler*. Intellect, 2011.

Soares, Andre. "Billy Wilder + Charles Brackett: Old Hollywood's Top Screenwriting Team." Alt Film Guide, 2016.

Staggs, Sam. *Billy Wilder, Norma Desmond, and the Dark Hollywood Dream*. St Martin's Griffin, 2002.

Steffen-Fluhr, Nancy. "Palimpsest: The Double Vision of Exile," in Karen McNally, ed., *Billy Wilder: Movie-Maker*. Macfarland Publishing, 2011.

Teachout, Terry. "What Wilder Did to Brackett." *Commentary*, November 2014.

Tuska, Jon. *Dark Cinema*. Greenwood Press, 1984.

Vineberg, Steve. *High Comedy in American Movies.* Rowman & Littlefield, 2005.

Wilmington, Michael. "LACMA Marks Lubitsch Centenary." *Los Angeles Times*, May 29, 1992.

Zolotow, Maurice, *Billy Wilder in Hollywood*, Limelight Editions, 2004

INDEX